LETTERS OF MARY W. SHELLEY

(MOSTLY UNPUBLISHED)

WITH INTRODUCTION AND NOTES

BY

HENRY H. HARPER

PRINTED ONLY FOR MEMBERS OF

THE BIBLIOPHILE SOCIETY

BOSTON · MDCDXVIII

THE·PLIMPTON·PRESS
NORWOOD·MASS·U·S·A

LETTERS OF MARY SHELLEY

INTRODUCTION BY HENRY H. HARPER

THIS group of holograph letters written by the gifted Mary Shelley possesses a distinct interest and literary value apart from the fact that their author was the wife of the world-renowned Shelley, or that they refer in intimate terms to many well known literary personages, such as Keats, Byron, Lamb, Wordsworth and other luminaries of the early nineteenth century. Any letters that bring us into close touch with the atmosphere of these characters must of necessity inspire a certain interest; but these letters have a far greater value than as mere gossip about literary men, however entertaining that might be.

Mary Shelley first became widely known when as a girl of sixteen she ran away, in the early morning of July 28, 1814, with the now immortal poet, who was then unhappily married to Harriet Westbrook;

but at that time, aside from being the grandson of an English baronet, he had achieved comparatively little that gave promise of immortality. Four months earlier he had written to a friend, — "I have sunk into a premature old age of exhaustion which renders me dead to everything but the unenviable capacity of indulging the vanity of hope, and a terrible susceptibility to objects of disgust and hatred. . . . I live here like the insect that sports in a transient sunbeam, which the next cloud shall obscure forever." That one "hope" proved to be Mary, who apparently revived his spirits, for in the inspiring companionship of this talented girl he produced most of the work by which he so greatly enriched the world's literature. Considering the fact that Mary had been obliged to live under the same roof with her father, the nagging, parasitical William Godwin, and a stepmother who was not famed for her tenderheartedness, it is not surprising that she should have run away with somebody, or anybody.

In this exploit she was accompanied by the daughter of her stepmother, a beautiful young lady named Jane (afterwards known as Clare) Clairmont, who abandoned the same uncongenial home to go with Mary and Shelley. Shortly after this adventure William Godwin wrote to one of his creditors, John Taylor, as follows — "In the night of the 27th Mary and her sister Jane escaped from my house, and the next morning when I rose I found a letter on my dressing table informing me what they had done. . . . Jane we were, and still are, most anxious to recover immediately; and therefore after much deliberation it was agreed that Mrs. G[odwin] should set off after them by the evening's mail. She overtook them at Calais. I had made it a condition in suffering her to depart, that she should avoid seeing Shelley, who had conceived a particular aversion to her as a dangerous foe to his views, and might be capable of any act of desperation. Mrs. Godwin wrote to Jane the very moment she reached Calais, July 29, who came to her at a separate inn, spent the night with her, and promised to return with her to England the next morning. But when morning arrived she said she must see the fugitives for a few minutes, and in that interview all her resolutions were sub-

9

verted. Not the most earnest entreaties of a mother could turn her from her purpose; and on Sunday, July 31, Mrs. Godwin returned once more alone."[1]

Of this episode Mr. H. Buxton Forman says that "the meeting of these two revolutionized Shelley's very soul, so to speak, and by the agency of a grand passion such as he never for a moment had for Harriet, transformed the accomplished and rhetorical author of *Queen Mab* into the authentic and indubitable poet of *Alastor*."

The world's debt of gratitude to Mary Shelley can hardly be overestimated, for her influence upon the life and the work of Shelley was very marked throughout their entire eight years of mutual devotion, — the years of his productivity. She did not fall into the error, too common among young women, of assuming that she had "landed a man," and that she could hold him by her physical attractions alone. Instead, she applied herself at once to the task of improving her mind along lines congenial to him, as will be shown by the

[1] This letter appears to have eluded all the biographers. It is in the possession of Mr. William K. Bixby, and was printed, for the first time, so far as known, in the Tenth Year Book of The Bibliophile Society.

following extraordinary list of works that she read in the first year. Twenty-nine of these, in addition to twenty-three others, were read by Shelley in the same year.

LIST OF BOOKS READ IN 1815

Posthumous Works. 3 vols.
Sorrows of Werter
Don Roderick. By Southey
Gibbon's Decline and Fall. 12 vols.
Gibbon's Life and Letters. 1st Edition. 2 vols.
Lara
New Arabian Knights. 3 vols.
Corinna
Fall of the Jesuits
Rinaldo Rinaldini
Fontenelle's Plurality of Worlds
Hermsprong
Le Diable Boiteux
Man as he is
Rokeby
Ovid's Metamorphoses in Latin
Wordsworth's Poems

Spenser's Fairy Queen
Life of the Phillips
Fox's History of James II
The Reflector
Fleetwood
Wieland
First vol. of Systeme de la Nature
Castle of Indolence
Chatterton's Poems
Paradise Regained
Don Carlos
Lycidas
St. Leon
Shakespeare's Plays (part of which Shelley read aloud)
Burke's Account of Civil Society
Excursion
Pope's Homer's Illiad
Sallust
Micromejas
Peter Wilkins

11

Rousseau's Confessions
Leonora: a Poem
Émile
Milton's Paradise Lost
Life of Lady Hamilton
De 'Allemagne. By Madame de Staël
Three vols. of Barruet
Caliph Vathek
Nouvelle Heloise
Kotzebue's Account of his Banishment to Siberia
Waverley
Clarissa Harlowe
Robertson's History of America
Virgil
Tale of a Tub
Milton's Speech on Unlicensed Printing
Curse of Kehama

Madoc
La Bible Expliquée
Lives of Abelard and Heloise
The New Testament
Coleridge's Poems
Life of Chaucer
Canterbury Tales
Peruvian Letters
Voyages round the World
Plutarch's Lives
Two vols. of Gibbon
Ormond
Hugh Trevor
Labaume's History of the Russian War
Lewis's Tales
Castle of Udolpho
Guy Mannering
Charles XII., by Voltaire
Tales of the East

For a girl of sixteen to read and intelligently study such a prodigious mass of learning in the space of twelve months shows a degree of application and mental precocity almost beyond human comprehension. This was followed by the reading of more than a hundred other volumes in the English, Latin and Greek languages. Her ambition to keep pace with the mental development of the erudite Shelley never flagged for a moment, and in whatever field his quest of knowledge and inspiration carried him he found her, not at his heels, but by his side. To this end she delved into the study of various languages, and in an incredibly short time she acquired a considerable knowledge of Greek, Latin, and Italian. Painting, drawing, sculpture, and music also came within the scope of her studies; indeed anything and everything that served to bring her into closer mental touch with her Shelley — "My Shelley," she always called him. From Rome she wrote to Hunt: "We pass our days viewing the divinest statues in the world. . . . Besides our eternal visits to these divine objects, Clare is learning to sing, I painting, and S. is writing a poem,[1] so that the *belle arte* take up all our time." Together they wandered here and there through art galleries and amid inspiring historic scenes; they visited the Pantheon by moonlight and "saw the lovely sight of the moon appearing through the round

---

[1] The "poem" was doubtless *Prometheus Unbound*, Shelley's masterpiece, most of which was written amid the ruins of the Baths of Caracalla.

aperture above, and lighting the columns of the Rotunda with its rays. . . . We live surrounded by antiquity ruined and perfect, besides seeing the lovely pictures of your favorite Raphael." Together, also, they ascended Vesuvius, made excursions to Pompeii, Herculaneum, Paestum and other historic places.

If Mary Shelley had no other claim upon posterity than that of having been the constant helpmate of the poet while he wrote *The Cenci*, — suggested by her, — *Alastor*, and *Prometheus Unbound*, that alone would be sufficient;[1] but her helpfulness to him is by no means her only claim to recognition. From her talented mother — who died in giving her birth[2] — she in-

---

[1] In dedicating one of his greatest works to Mary, Shelley wrote the following beautiful lines: —

So now my summer-task is ended, Mary,
And I return to thee, mine own heart's home;
As to his Queen some victor Knight of Faëry,
Earning bright spoils for her enchanted dome;
Nor thou disdain, that ere my fame become
A star among the stars of mortal night
If it indeed may cleave its natal gloom,
Its doubtful promise thus I would unite
With thy beloved name, thou Child of love and light.

[2] Her mother, Mary Wallstonecraft, gained wide celebrity as the author of *A Vindication of the Rights of Women*. Her name and her work become well known in America. The

herited her sweet, persuasive nature and the literary instincts that produced *Frankenstein*, *Valperga*, *Lodore*, and other works; while as a letter writer her crisp, incisive style is attested by these intimate personal epistles to Mr. and Mrs. Hunt.

All of Mrs. Shelley's correspondence shows her to have been a keen observer, of unusual perceptive faculties, a critic of art, literature, the drama, and especially the opera. This is shown not only in the present correspondence, but is perhaps

following lines addressed by Shelley to Mary show his regard for her mother: —

They say that thou wert lovely from thy birth,
Of glorious parents, thou aspiring child.
I wonder not, for one then left the earth,
Whose life was like a setting planet mild
Which clothed thee in the radiance undefiled
Of its departing glory; still her fame
Shines on thee, through the tempest dark and wild
Which shakes these latter days, and thou canst claim
The shelter, from thy sin, of an immortal name.

In the manuscript Shelley put an asterisk at "thy sin" in the last line, referring to a line at the bottom, where he wrote — "The author of *An Enquiry Concerning Political Justice*," a book written by Mary's father, who had caused them so much annoyance. The reader is left to conjecture Shelley's meaning. Possibly he intended to write *sire*, but he certainly wrote it *sin*. Mary's father (Godwin), who, after begging money from Shelley through a third party, became highly insulted because Shelley sent a personal check made payable direct to him!

even more conspicuously illustrated in her letters to John Howard Payne, printed for the first time some years ago by The Bibliophile Society in a volume entitled *The Romance of Mary Shelley, John Howard Payne and Washington Irving.* Combining these qualities with a sympathetic, gentle, lovable nature which accorded perfectly with Shelley's ideals, it is reasonable to suppose that from such an environment he derived much inspiration and actual assistance in his remarkable literary achievements. What he might ultimately have become without her we do not know, and it would be fruitless to speculate; but with her we all know what he accomplished, and we know that genius, though generally supposed to be innate, requires the proper sort of nourishment to bring it into full flower, no less than a plant requires good soil and proper husbandry. A noted biographer has said of Shelley, "That he became what he did, is in great measure due to her."

The reading of the lives of Percy and Mary Shelley, from the time of the elopement on July 28, 1814, to the time when Shelley was drowned, on that eventful 8th of July, 1822, gives one a feeling somewhat akin to that of viewing a company of unfortunates struggling in a vast entanglement of briars, with the thorns set at such angles that no matter which way the victims turn, their flesh is torn on one side while being pricked on the other; and just as they appear to be emerging from one thicket they find themselves enmeshed in another.

From the very day of their elopement one calamity followed another in such rapid succession that their affairs became a veritable panorama of disasters, one pressing hard upon the heels of another, and oftentimes half a dozen or more overlapping, — reminding one of the troubles of Job. Little wonder that Shelley is said to have "found a peculiar attraction" in this biblical story! From one side they were eternally beset by all sorts of extortionate claims and demands upon their scanty income, from another side came a perpetual rain of scandalous criticism and vituperation, from another quarter came a succession of illness, poverty and bailiffs; then the necessity of constantly moving about hither and yon to escape arrest and

17

imprisonment for debts incurred at ruinous rates of interest in mitigating the financial distress of Godwin and others. Inside their own household Clare Clairmont, who seemed thrust upon them for life, unexpectedly gave birth to an infant as the result of a *liaison* with Lord Byron, thereby casting public suspicion upon Shelley himself, which he was unable to allay; then the deaths, one after another, of their three children, not to mention the never-ceasing slanders and importunities of Mary's impecunious father, William Godwin, who never suffered them to remain for more than a few days at a time in ignorance of some new financial difficulty of his own. Like a ship riding a storm-tossed sea, they emerged from one troublesome mélange only to find themselves plunged into another. Indeed it became a sort of habit with them during occasional brief periods of comparative calm to speculate on what new catastrophe was in store for them. If anything were lacking to disturb Shelley's equanimity it was amply supplied in the form of the most villainous charges, that he had shamelessly abused Mary, conducted his house as a brothel, ruined Clare Clair-

mont, was responsible for the suicide of
her sister Fanny, and was guilty of other
pusillanimous conduct, all of which was
equally annoying and repugnant to his
nature. He was so maliciously persecuted
and stigmatized publicly and privately that
finally, in broken health and depressed
spirits, he fled the country in disgust, never
to return.[1] Wherever they were, at home

[1] It is not to be wondered at that "the subject Shelley
loved best to dwell on was the image of one warring with the
Evil Principle." Nor is it surprising that the prejudice
against him operated as a barrier to any immediate public
recognition of his talents. He wrote to Mary from Ravenna,
— "My greatest content would be to desert all human
society . . . and retire with you and our child to a solitary
island in the sea, . . . and devote either to oblivion or to
future generations the overflowings of a mind which, timely
withdrawn from contagion, should be kept fit for no baser
object." That he did not give up in despair proves his
courage and the firmness of his purpose to write for "future
generations." He was excoriated and admonished by his
erstwhile friend Southey, the poet, then enjoying widespread
popularity, but whose present fame, as compared with that
of Shelley, may be likened to a tiny star in the glare of a
noonday sun. Shelley bore most of his insults in silence,
but stung by Southey's impertinence he was moved to retort
— "With what care do the most tyrannical Courts of Judica-
ture weigh evidence and surround the accused with protecting
forms; with what reluctance do they pronounce their cruel
and presumptuous decisions, compared with you! You
select a single passage out of a life otherwise not only spotless,
but spent in an impassioned pursuit of virtue, which looks
like a blot merely because I regulated my domestic arrangements without deferring to the notions of the vulgar."

or abroad, they lived constantly in the shadow of a deep gloom, with Pandora's Box—seemingly bottom upward—and the Sword of Damocles always suspended over their heads, both following them about as if attracted by some powerful magnet in their bodies. About the only bright or harmonious spot in their lives was their unalterable devotion to each other. If neither Shelley nor Mary had ever written a line, their experiences alone would have immortalized their names.

But amid all their sorrows and joys they read, read, read, incessantly. They simply devoured Livy, Gibbon, Tacitus, Sismondi, Plutarch, Plato, Dante, Spenser, Shakespeare, Milton, Montaigne, Rousseau, Horace, Vergil, Seneca, Sophocles, Euripides, Homer, Tasso, Theocritus, Chaucer, and dozens of others. On the day her first born died Mary recorded in her journal that in the evening she read *The Fall of the Jesuits*, and next day she read *Rinaldo Rinaldini!* With both of them, reading and study were the panacea for all ills, and they had them a-plenty, — the relaxation from all pleasures, which were indeed few. Through their multifarious troubles, however, they bore up with Spartanlike fortitude, and are said to have disguised their feelings "under a mask of cheerfulness." What a pity that Shelley did not follow his *Mask of Anarchy* with a sequel entitled, *The Mask of Cheerfulness!* If any man, woman or child should imagine that he or she has a case of the Troubles, a reading of the Lives of Mary [1] and Percy Shelley [2] will instantly dispel any such illusion. And yet, as soil fertilized by the most disagreeable substances sends forth the most delicious fruits, so from the lives of these two unfortunate beings, beset by nearly every painful affliction known to mankind, sprang the most delicious literary fruits known to modern times.

That Shelley was a great poet is a fact now recognized by everyone; that Mary Shelley was the source from which he drew much of his inspiration is a fact less widely known; but still less known is the fact that these two soul mates, even in times when their funds were at a low ebb, and the tides of their own troubles rolled

[1] *The Life and Letters of Mary Wallstonecraft Shelley*, by Mrs. Julian Marshall, London, 1889.

[2] *The Life of Percy Bysshe Shelley*, by Edward Dowden, LL.D., London, 1887.

highest, were ever alert to the needs and sufferings of the poor. Theirs was not the beneficence of the Lord and Lady Bountiful type, but what they lacked in amount was more than made up for by the sympathy and zest with which they gave such as they had to give. They practised the principles that Shelley so assiduously preached, — the Brotherhood of Man. They worked continuously among the poor, not by emissaries, but by personal visits from cottage to cottage. When they resided at Marlow, "if they happened to be absent from home," says a biographer, "the bag of coins was left in Mrs. Maddocks' hands, to be dispensed at the end of the week by her." Mrs. Maddocks wrote to Lady Shelley in 1859: "Every spot is sacred that he visited; he was a gentleman that seldom took money about with him, and we received numerous little billets, written sometimes on the leaf of a book, to pay the bearer the sum he specified, sometimes as much as half a crown; and one day he came home without shoes, saying that he had no paper, so he gave the poor man his shoes." On December 29, 1817, when almost destitute himself, he bought twenty heavy blankets and nearly fifty dollars' worth of sheeting which were distributed among the neighborhood's poor.

In Italy, says one who knew him there, "Shelley's constant habits of benevolence did not abate in this wild and half-inhabited region; whenever there was sickness in a house within his range, there would he be found, nursing and advising."

Perhaps the immolation of these two souls by their contemporary world was, after all, a blessing in disguise, since it drew them closer together and caused them to seek their temporal happiness in each other's companionship and in acts of benevolence to those beneath their caste; while their spiritual labors were destined for the enchantment of future and more appreciative generations.

Mary Shelley occupied the extremely difficult position of being married to a literary genius, who belonged to the ideal rather than the real world, even if in the capacity of buffer for trouble-makers he seemed to belong to any- and everybody. In his quest for ideals he displayed the same rare intuition in the selection of his second mate that he exhibited in his literary work, and after equipping himself with this important desideratum he set to his task in dead earnest, and in eight years he made for himself a name that will endure to the end of civilization. Having hitched her chariot to a comet she took the risk of a hard fall, but notwithstanding her trying position, with the generous accompaniment of ills and ailments, she made for both him and herself more genuine connubial joy than is allotted to the average individual in the full span of an ordinary lifetime. She entered into his life with the fixed determination to succeed, and as a successful physician must needs study the nerve forces and arteries of the human body, so she studied the vagaries and needs of the man of her choice and fitted herself to fill every niche in his life. She abandoned friends, home, country and everything, not for love, but for Shelley. Shelley and his happiness became her life, her earthly God, her all, and if she pleased him and helped him in attaining his ideals it mattered not if the whole world anathematized her and branded her a social outcast. In Paris, ten days after the elopement, Shelley wrote in his journal, — "Mary especially seems insensible to all future evil. She feels as if our love would alone suffice to resist the invasions of calamity!" Nothing daunted, nothing mattered with her but Shelley. She determined to make herself as indispensable to him and his work as fire is necessary to a steam engine, or a dynamo to an electric light — and by dint of hard work she succeeded. In running away with him, a married man, she was prompted by no spirit of lewdness, romance or adventure; she was intelligent, far beyond her years, and wide awake to the consequences; it was no light or frivolous affair; it was a serious business with her; she knew they would both be ostracized and penniless, but that was of no relative importance; she had an aim in life, and that was to help Shelley in the fulfillment of his laudable ambition. The fault-finding world could go hang; if she accomplished her aim they would soon enough be fawning at his feet, and his ultimate triumph would be her sufficient recompense. With her inherent talents and her serious studious nature she would doubtless have made for herself a greater name than she did with Shelley's

25

fame overshadowing hers, but Shelley's renown was of far more concern to her than her own. After Shelley's death she wrote to her friend Mrs. Gisborne: "I would not change my situation as his widow with that of the most prosperous woman in the world."

From neither of her parents did Mary inherit any dogmatic ideas affecting intolerable marriage relations; therefore she suffered no scruples of conscience in accepting Shelley's love, especially after she had taken at its surface value the assurance that his wife had proved false to her marriage vows. By an onerous decree of the law he might belong to another, but she felt that by a higher law his love belonged to her, and that she was committing no crime in accepting what someone had cast aside and did not own or care for. A horse tied to a stake would soon consume all the verdure within its reach and then perish of hunger; there could be no offence either against God or any just-minded human being in rescuing it from such a fate. Shelley was so constituted that a loving, congenial companion was no less needful than food and drink to the fulfillment of his happiness and his ideals; and she did not intend that he should lack any stimulus that it was within her power to supply, as long as she lived — and he never did. Her one dream of happiness was to make him happy, regardless of all else, and so far as is known she never sought in any way to promote her own well being except in so far as it should be reflected from his own. Whatever may have been charged against her by her detracters they never found cause to accuse her of a single act or thought disloyal to Shelley, either during his lifetime or thereafter.

"What a strange life mine has been!" she wrote in her journal; "Love, youth, fear, and fearlessness led me early from the regular routine of life, and I united myself to this being, who, not one of *us*, though like to us, was pursued by numberless miseries and annoyances, in all of which I shared. . . . But that is gone. His voice can no longer be heard; the earth no longer receives the shadow of his form; annihilation has come over the earthly appearance of the most gentle creature that ever yet breathed this air; and I am still here — still thinking, existing, all but hoping."

And again, on November 10, following Shelley's death: — "What a delight it is to be associated with a superior! Mine own Shelley! the sun knows of none to be likened to you — brave, wise, noble-hearted, full of learning, tolerance, and love. Love! what a word for me to write! Yet, my miserable heart, permit me yet to love, — to see him in beauty, to feel him in beauty, to be interpenetrated by the sense of his excellence; and thus to love singly, eternally, ardently, and not fruitlessly; for I am still his — still the chosen one of that blessed spirit — still vowed to him for ever and ever!"

LETTERS OF MARY SHELLEY

The first few letters in this collection were written after Mary's marriage to Shelley, and at a period when there was a comparative lull in their tumultuous affairs; but it was of short duration.

Marlow, March 2nd, 1817.

My dear Mrs. Hunt —

It is said that our days for letter writing fade as we grow older (and I, you know, am an old woman[1]) and for some time I felt it so myself. I know not how it is, but ever since I have left you I think I could write all day long and wish to hear as often from you all. I wish at one time to describe our house to you, but that is useless as you will soon see it. It is indeed a delightful place, very fit for the luxurious literati who enjoy a good library, a beautiful garden and a delightful country surrounding it.

But I meant this to be a letter of business

[1] She was then nineteen, but in the preceding two and a half years she had experienced more troubles and joys than fall to the lot of most women grown old in years.

29

as there are two or three things that I am
impertinent enough to imagine your kindness warrants my asking you to do for me.

First. — If you have not sent my clothes
do not wait for Shelley's departure but let
me have them without delay.

Secondly. — Will you take the trouble
to furnish me with a little stock of haber-
dashery, as I cannot well get it here.
This includes — a quantity of White Chapel
needles, balls of cotton of all sizes, tapes,
some black sewing silk and silk of other
colours, pins, a pair of large and one of
small scissors and any other articles of the
same nature that you may deem necessary.
Will you also get from Clare all the clothes
she has got of Will's.

And now tell me how your headaches
are and if anything has disturbed you
since our departure. If nothing new has
happened, pray remember sufficient for the
day is the evil thereof; and do not disturb
yourself by prognostics. This may be a
difficult, but I believe it is an attainable
art and surely it is very desirable. Believe
me my poor Mary Anne, all your fears
and sorrows shall fly when you behold the
blue skies and bright sun of Marlow and

feel its gentle breezes (not winds) on your cheeks. We enjoy in this town a most delightful climate — and rivers, woods and flowering fields make no contemptible appendage to a bright sky.

How does Clare go on — is she content and happy? and is her babe[1] thriving? My Willy is cutting some more teeth, which occasions a little fretting, but upon the whole he goes on very well.

Give my love to Miss K. and the children.

Affectionately yours,

MARY W. S.

Will you be so kind as to enclose in your next letter a paper of accounts that I gave you to take care of for me.

We do not mean to take Marlow servants — Can you contrive that I should see some while in London?

Marlow, March 2nd, 1817

Dear Hunt —

Shelley and Peacock[2] have started a

[1] This was the child Allegra, of which Lord Byron was the father. For a short time after the birth of her babe Clare lived apart from the Shelleys, but she afterwards returned to them with her infant, which was later sent to Lord Byron at Venice.

[2] Thomas Love Peacock, author of *Palmyra* and other

question which I do not esteem myself
wise enough to decide upon; and yet as
they seem determined to act on it I wish
them to have the *best advice*.   As a prelude
to this you must be reminded that Hampden
was of Buck's and our two worthies want
to be his successors, for which reason they
intend to refuse to pay the taxes as illegally
imposed.   What effect will this have, and
ought they to do it, is the question?   Pray
let me know your opinion.

Our house is very political as well as
poetical and I hope you will acquire a
fresh spirit for both when you come here.
You will have plenty of room to indulge
yourself in, and a garden which will deserve
your praise when you see it — flowers,
trees and shady banks.   Ought we not to
be happy? and so indeed we are, in spite
of the Lord Chancellor[1] and the Suspension
Act.   But I assure you we hope for a great
addition to it when you are so kind as to
come to us.   By the bye, could you not
come down with Shelley and stay only a

Poems. His letters from Shelley while in Italy are gems of
literature.

[1] This was but a few days after Lord Chancellor Eldon
rendered his decree, denying Shelley the custody of his two
children, a boy and a girl, by his first wife.

day or two, just to view your future abode? It would give me great delight to see you and I think the *tout ensemble* would give you some pleasure.

But for all this I know you will not come; but if one or two would — Mrs. Hunt, for instance, would lose her headache, I am quite certain in three minutes.

I have not yet seen the *Examiner*, but when I do I shall judge if you have been disturbed since we left you. The present state of affairs is sufficient to rouse anyone, I should suppose, except (as I wish to be contemptuous) a weekly politician. This, however, as I have not seen your paper, is rather cats' play — if you have been *good* it will pass off very well, but if you have not I shall be very sorry; but I send it depending that you have pleased yourself this week.

We will hasten everything to have you down and you shall be indulged in sophas, hair brushes and hair brushers to your heart's content; but then in return you and Mrs. Hunt must leave off calling me Mrs. S[helley] for I do not half like the name.[1]

[1] As a matter of fact, she was always prouder of the name than of all else in the world, excepting only Shelley himself.

Remember us all with kindness, and believe me

Your very sincere friend,

MARY W. S.

Let me know if you have been at peace since our departure, and if you all have taken advantage of these fine days to improve your health and spirits by exercise. S[helley] has been very well. In one of the parcels will you send down the hair that you have got for me.

Do you know if you could get in town a small ivory casket in which I could put those memorials?

Marlow, March 5, 1817

My dear Mrs. Hunt —

I have received the parcel and your very kind letter this evening, and I thank [you] for the latter a thousand times. All my clothes, however, are not come; no gowns being in the parcel, which I want very much. But I suppose they will come by Shelley.

A spencer that fits Mary would I think just do for Will. I wish it to button

What she doubtless meant was that she did not like such formality between intimate friends.

34

behind. I would rather also that it should be crimson, as that soils less than scarlet.

I have written a long letter to Hunt and as you and he are one, and as my affection for you both is, I believe, pretty nearly equal (if you will not be jealous), perhaps you will excuse a long letter as I am rather prest for time — not but that I have plenty to say.

But I must not forget to praise my good girl for her resolutions and exhort her to fortify them by every forcible argument I know of. And indeed to see or know of the content and pleasure Hunt feels when you and Bessy agree must be enough to make you *appear* so at least; especially as with Hunt every symptom of generosity touches him deeply when anything that looks (in his opinion) towards the other side of the question makes him angry. Cultivate his affection and cherish and enjoy his society and I am sure my dear Mary Anne will find her prospects clear very sensibly.

Our furniture will arrive Saturday morning and if Hunt will let me use a selfish argument you would be very *useful* to me. But on second thought do not let him see this ugly sentence, as your greatest use must be towards him; and besides he does not like being teazed.

William[1] is very well. How is your little one after being weaned? Give my love to all the children.

Do not fear Hunt's boldness. I do not think that that does any harm if he steers clear of societies and libels, and what he says is not libelous certainly.

I am glad to hear of the health of Clare's babe; poor girl she *must* be lonely.

Shelley mentions Mrs. G's[2] favour — is she not an odious woman!

I hope we shall see you very soon and this air will certainly drive away all headaches.

Your affectionate friend,

MARY W. S.

I wrote to Shelley today; if he had departed before the letter arrived, burn it.

Marlow, March 5th, 1817
1 o'clock

My dear Hunt —

Although you mistook me in thinking that I wish you to write about politics in

[1] Mary's child.   [2] Mrs. Godwin, Mary's stepmother.

36

your letters to me, as such a thought was in fact far from me, yet I cannot help mentioning your last week's *Examiner*, as its boldness gave me extreme pleasure. I am very glad to find that you wrote the leading article, which I had doubted as there was no significant hand. But though I speak of this do not fear that you will be teazed by me on these subjects when we enjoy your company at Marlow. When there, you shall never be serious when you wish to be merry; and have as many nuts to crack as there are words in the petitions to Parliament for reform. A tremendous promise!

Have you never felt in your succession of nervous feelings one single disagreeable truism gain a painful possession of your mind and keep it for some months? A year ago, I remember my private hours were all made bitter by reflections on the certainty of death — and now the flight of time has the same power over me. Every thing passes and one is hardly conscious of enjoying the present before it becomes the past. I was reading the other day the letters of Gibbon. He entreats Lord Sheffield to come with all his family to visit

37

him at Lausanne, and dwells on the pleasure such a visit will occasion. There is a little gap in the date of his letters and then he complains that his solitude is made more irksome by their having been there and departed. So will it be with us in a few months when you will all have left Marlow. But I will not indulge this gloomy feeling. The sun shines brightly and we shall be very happy in our garden this summer.

Do you know that I am wicked enough to wish to run away from this place and to come to Hampstead until Saturday, as our furniture does not arrive until then, and Mrs. Peacock [1] is not so bright and agreeable a companion as my poor dear Mary Anne; and to tell you a little truth I do not like Peacock a millionth part so well as I do you. But this freak must not extend further than my fancy. The conversations I should promise myself must dwindle into letters and the music will be dissipated long before it reaches me — this being an Irishism, and as it is I will put bye my writing until I am in a merrier mood more according with yours — for I

[1] Peacock's mother. He afterwards married.

had a dream tonight of the dead being alive, which has affected my spirits.[1]

I send this letter in a parcel to Clare containing her music — among which there are two or three songs that I should like you to learn — the Ranz des Vaches and the Marseillaise hymn with the French words which Clare will teach you to pronounce if necessary. Now do not think this in [sic] in me — for it is taken from your own report, as I never heard you speak two words of French in my life. But when I see you, for convenience sake you must either learn that or Italian, that we may not always shock one another with our vernacular tongue — a thing Molière's philosopher could not endure.

I suppose you have not been to the opera. Peacock will be disappointed by the alteration this week as he wished very much to see Figaro. When a child I used to like going to the play exceedingly; and more from association than anything else I liked it afterwards. But I went seldom,

---

[1] Mary probably refers here to her first child, which died a few days after its birth. The second was Clara, the third, William, and the fourth Percy, who alone survived.

39

principally from feeling the delight I once felt wearing out; but this last winter it has been renewed and I again look forward to going to the theatre as a great treat quite exquisite enough, as of old, to take away my appetite for dinner. A play, in fact, is nothing unless you have people you like with you, and then it is an exquisite pleasure.

Take care of yourself. Give my love to Miss K. and tell her to be good and I will love her.

Adieu. — Be not angry with us for being such new friends, for I like you too well to wish you [to] forget me, or to be other than as I am,

Affectionately yours,

MARINA

Marlow, March 18th, 1817

My dear Friend —

We have not received any letter from you, but have heard from Clare that your friend Mr. Horace Smith[1] is ill. I hope, however, that when you receive this you

---

[1] In the following October Horace Smith loaned Shelley two hundred and fifty pounds. He became Shelley's close friend, and figured prominently in his after life.

will find him so far restored as to free you from anxiety. The *Examiner* of this week also says a great deal for you. I am glad to see you write much and well as it shows your mind is at peace. I am now writing in the library of our house in which we are to sleep tonight for the first time. It is very comfortable and expectant of its promised guests. The statues are arrived and every thing is getting on. Come then, dear good creatures, and let us enjoy with you the beauty of the Marlow sun and the pleasant walks that will give you all health, spirits and *industry*.

Hogg [1] is at present a visitor of Peacock. I do not like him and I think he is more disagreeable than ever. I would not have him come every week to disturb our peace by his ill humour and noise for all the world. Both of the menagerie [2] were very much scandalized by the praise and sonnet

[1] This was Thomas Jefferson Hogg. He afterwards married Jane Williams, whose husband was drowned with Shelley in 1822.

[2] Mary here becomes playful. The "menagerie," of course, consisted of *Peacock* and *Hogg*. The publication of Keats' sonnet in the *Examiner* is said to have been one of the first recognitions of his genius. Keats was one of Shelley's few loyal friends who did not desert him, and their friendship was memorialized in Shelley's *Adonais*.

of Keats, and mean, I believe, to petition against the publication of any more. It was transferred to the *Chronicle* — Is that an honour?

I have a word or two to say to Mrs. Hunt, and not having any more paper in the house tonight, and it being too late to get more, I must with this country excuse cut short my letter to you. Write and if you wish it you shall have a long answer.

Your affectionate friend,

MARINA

It is very impertinent to give the lady the last place, but I did not know how little paper I had when I began.

My dear Mary Anne —

My little red box is not yet arrived and I am in agony. I hope it is sent; if not, pray send it with the rest of the things mentioned in the list. What about a servant? If you get one let her be a *good cook*, for I think we must have two and I can easily get a housemaid. Do not entirely agree with one until you let me know. Have you given Clare Lord B's letters yet? She mentions that you had not, in a letter we had from her today. They will give her so much pleasure.

William is very well and can now walk alone, but I am afraid his teeth will put him back again. How is Swynburn and the rest of your babies? Kiss them for me and give my love to Miss Kent.

I hope Hunt will criticise *Melincourt next week*. Have you been to see Cymbeline or the Opera?

Take care of yourself, my dear girl, I long to see you all down here and hope, for Hunt's sake, that we shall by that time have received the long with-held hairbrush.[1]

Most affectionately yours,
MARY W. S.

Shelley sends his love to you all.

[1] Soon after this letter was written Mary visited her old home, then the Hunts came to make a protracted visit to Marlow, so that no other letters appear to have been written to either of them for more than a year, when Mary next wrote them from Italy. In the meantime, on the 27th of May, Clare returned, with her baby, to take up her residence with the Shelleys at Marlow, and afterwards accompanied them to Italy, where the child was placed in Byron's care. Clare was a vivacious, likable girl; she relinquished the child to its father's keeping because, she said, she wanted it to become an object of his affection and to receive an education becoming the child of an English nobleman.

43

Milan, April, 1818

My dear Friends —

We have at length arrived in Italy.
After winding for several days through
vallies and crossing mountains and passing
Cenis we have arrived in this land of blue
skies and pleasant fields. The fruit trees
all in blossom and the fields green with
the growing corn. Hunt already says —
I should like this. Indeed as we passed
along the mountainous districts of Savoy
we often said — Hunt would not like this;
but the first evening that we arrived in
Italy every thing appeared changed. We
arrived at Susa the first Italian town at
the foot of Cenis about six in the evening
and Shelley and I went to look at a tri-
umphal arch that had been erected to the
honour of Augustus. It was nearly in
perfect preservation and most beautifully
surrounded by mountains. The path under
it was preserved in beautiful order a green
lane covered with flowers, a pretty Italian
woman went with us and plucked us a
nosegay of violets.

Italy appears a far more civilised place
than France; you see more signs of cultivation and work and you meet multitudes of

peasants on the road driving carts drawn by the most beautiful oxen I ever saw. They are of a delicate dove colour with eyes that remind you of, and justify the Homeric epithet, *ox-eyed Juno*. In France you might travel many miles and not meet a single creature. The inns are infinitely better and the bread, which is uneatable in France, is here the finest and whitest in the world. There is a disconsolate air of discomfort in France that is quite wretched. In Italy we breathe a different air and every thing is pleasant around us. At Turin we went to the opera; it was a little shabby one and except the lights on the stage the house was in perfect darkness. There were two good singers and these the people heard, but during the rest of the time you were deafened by the perpetual talking of the audience. We have been also at the opera of Milan. The house is nearly as large as that of London and the boxes more elegantly fitted up. The scenery and decorations much more magnificent. Madame Camporeri is the Prima Donna but she was ill and we did not hear her. Indeed we heard nothing, for the people did not like the opera, which had been repeated every night for these three weeks; so not one air was heard. But the ballet was infinitely magnificent. It was (strange to say) the story of Othello; but it was rather a tragic pantomime than a ballet. There was no dancer like Mlle. Mélanie, but the whole was in a finer style. The corps de ballet is excellent and they throw themselves into groups fit for a sculptor to contemplate. The music of the ballet was very fine and the gestures striking. The dances of many performers which are so ill-executed with us are here graceful to the extreme. The theatre is not lighted and the ladies dress with bonnets and pelisses, which I think a great pity. The boxes are dear, but the pit — in which none but respectable people are admitted — is only eighteen pence, so that our amusement is very cheap.

I like this town. The ladies dress very simply and the only fault of their costume is the length of their petticoats; so that Marianne's pretty feet would be quite hid. We think, however, of spending the summer on the banks of the lake of Como, which is only twenty miles from here. Shelley's health is infinitely improved and the rest of the chicks are quite well. How are you all? And how do you like Don Garcia and il Barbiere di Seviglia? We half expected a letter to have arrived before us, but the posts travel very slowly here. Let us have long letters. Do you see Peacock and is he in despair? Remember me to all friends and kiss your babes for me.

I almost forgot to mention that we spent one day at thirty miles from Genoa. Elise's Mother and father-in-law and little girl came to see her. Aimée is very beautiful, with eyes something like, but sweeter, than William's — a perfect shaped nose and a more beautiful mouth than her Mother's, expressive of the greatest sensibility.

Adieu, my dear Hunt and Marianne. La Prima Donna sends her affectionate remembrances, and Shelley his love.

Most affectionately yours,
MARY W. SHELLEY

Direct to us —

Mess. Marietti — Banquers
Milano.
Italie.
Tell Ollier[1] that S. has not received his

[1] Ollier was Shelley's publisher.

parcel, but that he can send the proofs to Peacock for revision.

We left several things at our lodgings in Great Russel St. to be sent you — among the rest have you received William's service? If not, have kindness to enquire for it; for I should be very sorry that it should be lost. Shelley wishes you to call at the first jeweller's on the left hand side of the way in New Bond St. as you enter it from Oxford St. where we bought Marianne's broach.

Shelley left a ring to be mended and forgot to call for it. Tell Peacock to send Beppo and some pins and sealing wax with the first parcel — these things are so bad here.

Leghorn, May 13, 1818

My dear Friends —

We have been many weeks absent from England and we have had no letter from you. I hope, however, that there is a letter on the road and that this letter will only make you say — "Have they not yet had our letter?" and not — "Indeed I must write soon." We have, as you may perceive by the date of my letter, travelled farther south since I last wrote. We have passed through a country which would be the delight of Hunt — beautiful hedges blooming with hawthorn in flower and roses. Beautiful lanes are bounded by these and the cornfields are planted with rows of trees round which the vines twist themselves and are festooned from tree to tree so as to form the most pleasant leafy alleys in the world. After travelling several days through a country like this, blooming and fertile like a perpetual garden we came to the Apennines which we crossed in a most violent wind so that Clare was very much afraid that the carriage would be blown over. Here we quitted the scene which would be so pleasant to Hunt, but we found it again in the vale of the Arno along the banks of the river where nothing was wanting to the beauty of the scene but that the river should be capable of reflecting its banks; but unfortunately it is too muddy. Pisa is a dull town situated on the banks of the Arno; it has a fine cathedral, but not to be compared to that of Milan; and a tower which has been so shaken by an earthquake that it leans many feet on one side. Its gallery of pictures or whatever it contains we did

49

not see, putting that off till our return to the town. One thing, however, which disgusted me so much that I could never walk in the streets except in misery was that criminals condemned to labour work publickly in the streets, *heavily* ironed in pairs with a man with a gun to each pair to guard against their escape. These poor wretches look sallow and dreadfully wretched and you could get into no street but you heard the clanking of their chains.

I think this circumstance made us quit Pisa sooner than we otherwise should, and we came here to Leghorn to present a letter to a friend. We shall stay here, however, but a short time, for we intend to pass the summer at Florence. The people that we know here have been many years in Italy and have seen a great deal of the society in the principal towns here. There seems to be a very pleasant way of going on here if the members that compose the company are as agreeable as is their manner of visiting. One lady keeps open house in the evening and the rest resort to her. There are no refreshments and the English complain that they do not know what to do when they come in, for there is no appearance of receiving visits; for the company instead of assembling altogether are dispersed in parties about the room. They told us that whenever you call at an Italian house the servant always puts her head out of the window and demands *chi è*, whatever time of day or night it may be. The proper answer to this question is *amici*, but those people [who] do not know the proper reply are terribly puzzled to know what to answer to this *chi è* which meets them at every corner. One of their friends visiting a house after having been kept a long time in the street while they were screaming *chi è* to him from the window and he was exhausting all answers to them but the right one — at length made his way to the stairs which — as they always are in Italy — were dark, and as he was groping along, the mistress of the house called out *chi è* and the poor man quite confounded — not recognising the voice — called out, "Bruta bestia, andate al diavolo!" and rushed out of the house.

This town is a noisy mercantile one and we intend soon to quit it. It cannot be compared to Milan, which was a very pleasant city, large and populous yet quiet. There is no opera, and there was an excellent one at Milan. Particularly one singer who is famous in all Italy, of the name of David. He has a tenor voice and sings in a softer and sweeter way than you ever hear in England. In Italy, except the first night or two, you can never hear anything of the opera except some favourite airs; for the people make it a visiting place and play cards and sup in the boxes, so you may guess that the murmur of their voices rises far above the efforts of the singers. But they became silent to hear some of David's songs which, hardly at all accompanied, stole upon the ear like a murmur of waters, while Madame Camporeri ran up the octaves beside him in a far different manner.

You will be pleased to hear that Shelley is much better than he was. I suppose you all in England go on as you did when we left you, but I should like to know how all your little babes are. Do you see much of Peacock? And tell me if you go often to the opera and if any changes have taken place in that singing Paradise. We are the same as we were except that before we left Milan Alba [1] was sent to Venice, where they dress her in little trousers trimmed with lace, and treat her like a little Princess.

There lives here in Leghorn, and we are going to see her, an aunt of Mary Anne's favourite Mrs. Haydon — that Hero de se who has lately sent her over his bust in marble and promises to come and see her when his picture is finished; but you [know] when that will be, or rather you do not know as it goes on in the same manner as Penelope's web. He writes long letters to his relations here and I fancy they think him a little God.

What weather have you in England? Here it is very pleasant although not so hot as I expected; but we have peas and strawberries for dinner and I fancy you will not have them for another month. But this place is cooler than more inland towns on account of its vicinity to the sea, which is here like a lake without tides, blue and tranquil.

Shelley and Clare send their love.

[1] Allegra, Clare's child. Byron first placed her with some friends of his, then in a convent, where, on April 19, 1822, she died of typhus fever. "You may judge," wrote Mary to Mrs. Gidbourne, "of what was Clare's first burst of grief and despair."

Adieu, my dear Hunt and Marianne. May Æsculapius keep you in health, which prayer I have no doubt he will hear if you do not remain at home so much as you used.

Most affectionately yours,

MARY W. SHELLEY

Corso, Rome, March 12th, 1819

My dear Marianne —

You must have thought my silence long, between our letters from Lucca and those from Naples. I wrote you a long one from Venice, but the laudable love of gain (*buscare* as they call it — i.e., gaining their livelihood) which burns with zealous heat in the breast of every Italian caused the hotel keeper to charge the postage and to throw the letter into the fire together with several others. I wrote to you soon after the death of my little girl, which event I dare say Peacock has mentioned. We quitted Naples about a fortnight ago with great regret. The country is the divinest in the world, and as spring was just commencing it appeared that we left it when we just began to value it. But Rome repays for every thing. How you would

like to be here! We pass our days in
viewing the divinest statues in the world.
You have seen the casts of most of them,
but the originals are infinitely superior,
and besides you continually see some new
one of heavenly beauty that one never
saw before. There is an Apollo — it is
Shelley's favourite — in the Museum of
the Capitol. He is standing leaning back
with his feet crossed — one arm supports
a lyre, the other hand holds the instrument
to play on it and his head is thrown back
as he is in the act of being inspired and
the expression of his countenance, especially the lower part, is more beautiful
than you can imagine. There are a quantity of female figures in the attitude of
the Venus di Medici, generally taller and
slimmer than that plump little woman,
but I dare not say so graceful although I
do not see how they can be surpassed.
There is a Diana hunting — her dress
girded about her — she has just let fly an
arrow and watches its success with eagerness and joy. Nothing can be more vener-
able than the aspects of the statues of the
river Gods that abound here. Indeed it is
a scene of perpetual enchantment to live

55

in this thrice holy city; for add to these statues beautiful pictures and the fragments of magnificent architecture that meet your eye at every turn as you walk from one street to another.

The other evening we visited the Pantheon by moonlight and saw the lovely sight of the moon appearing through the round aperture above and lighting the columns of the Rotunda with its rays. But my letter would never be at an end if I were to try tell a millionth part of the delights of Rome — but it has such an effect on me that my past life before I saw it appears a blank; and now I begin to live. In the churches you hear the music of heaven and the singing of Angels.

But how are you all this time, my dear girl? And how are all your children? We were very much amused by some *Examiners* that we received in Peacock's parcel, although they were very old. We had Hunt's letter at Naples, pressing all his doubts and difficulties about the proposed [word undecipherable.] I am afraid indeed that you will [word undecipherable — magazine?] impracticable although you both be infinitely delighted. At Naples there is a delightful opera, although I do not know how you would like the Italian mode of managing it. They play the same opera for a year together and nothing is listened to of it except the favourite airs. Nothing is heard in Italy now but Rossini, and he is no favourite of mine. He has some pretty airs, but they say that when he writes a good thing he goes on copying it in all his succeeding operas for ever and ever. He composes so much that he cannot always be called on for something pretty and new.

Shelley is suffering his cure; he is teazed very much by the means but it certainly does him a great deal of good. William speaks more Italian than English. When he sees anything he likes he cries, "O Dio che bella!"

He has quite forgotten French for Elise [1] has left us. She married a rogue of an Italian servant that we had, and turned

[1] This was Mary's nursemaid, whom she befriended, and was repaid by the rankest perfidy. Her rogue of a husband afterwards attempted to extort money from Shelley by blackmail. He circulated the report in Italy that Shelley was the father of Clare's child, and caused no end of annoyance. Apparently Mary was not much given to complaining and detailing her troubles, for these letters give but little intimation of the inconveniences they suffered.

Catholic. Venice quite spoiled her and she appears in the high road to be as Italian as any of them. She has settled at Florence. Milly stays with us and goes on very well, except that during her exile her tender affection for *everything* English makes her in love with every Englishman that she meets.

Adieu, my dear Marianne. What modelling are you about? In stone or in what materials? I dare say you wont understand this. Adieu; keep yourself as well as you can and do not forget us.

Ever yours affectionately,

MARY W. SHELLEY

Shelley and Clare desire, with me, a thousand kind loves to Hunt and Bessy. Do you ever see Hogg? How he would scream and beat his sides at all the fine things in Rome! It is well that he is not [here] or he would have broken many a rib in his delights, or at least bruised them sorely.

Rome, Tuesday, April 6th, 1819
My dear Hunt —
Your long kind letter was very welcome to us, for it told us a little about you after

a long ignorance. You seem in good spirits and I hope this is not mere appearance and that every thing is well with you; and that at least you see the end of your difficulties. To tell you the truth, both Shelley and I thought that we left you free and had easy minds upon that score. So you still remember us and wish us back to England — and for your sake I wish that we were there; but I fear on our return to be enveloped not only in a bodily but a mental cloudy atmosphere whose simoonic wind sometimes contrives to reach us even in this country of sunshine. So we have determined — and very soon we shall not be able to change our determination — to stay here another year. In a couple of months we shall return to Naples where circumstances will keep us a long time and we shall be in Rome again at this time next year. You cannot come, you say; indeed I always feared that you could not, but you would like Italy very much. So if you feel inclined, some cold day next autumn take ship and come and find us on the shores of the bay of Naples enjoying a brighter sun than ever peers through the mists of your England.

I suppose that Peacock shows you Shelley's letters, so I need not describe those objects which delight us so much here. We live surrounded by antiquity, ruined and perfect, besides seeing the lovely pictures of your favourite Raphael who is the Prince, or rather God, of painting (I mean a heathen God, not a bungling modern divinity); and there are delightful painters besides him. Guido would be a great favourite of yours. You would not like Domenichino so well; he is so fond of painting that scapegoat of all that is shrivelled and miserable in human nature, Saint Jerolymo, but there are some very beautiful pictures of his. And then you know Rome is stuffed with the loveliest statues in the world — a much greater number than one has any idea of until one sees them, and most of them in the most perfect state. Besides our eternal visits to these divine objects, Clare is learning singing, I painting, and S. is writing a poem, so that the *belle arte* take up all our time. Swiny ought to be here to see the statues. We took our Will-man [1] to the Vatican and he was delighted with the Goats and the

[1] Their child, William.

Cavalli, and dolefully lamented over the man votto, which is his kind of language.

Your account of your nephew Henry interested us very much; it shows a very generous nature to undertake the cause of the absent, especially one so little known as Shelley is to him. Pray convey Shelley's thanks to him and let us know if his health is improved. We must thank you also for your delicacy about meeting the Turners. These people are very strange; but I always understood that their distaste to us originated with Alfred Boinville and he it seems is not of the present party; but Turner [1] is a bad envious man and a slanderer, so if we saw them we should at least keep a kind of barrier in the way of intimacy. Mrs. Boinville is a very delightful woman but has the unhappy knack of either forgetting or appearing to forget her friends as soon as they turn their backs.

You seem certain that Southey did not write the number in the *Quarterly*,[2] but if

[1] This was perhaps the person through whom Godwin had extorted money from Shelley before he became married to Mary.

[2] In April, 1819, the *Quarterly Review* contained the following scathing article on *The Revolt of Islam*: —

"In the enthusiasm of youth, indeed," wrote the reviewer,

61

he spares us in print he does not in conversation as we have good authority to know, and that he speaks in the grossest manner — but this is all nothing.

"a man like Mr. Shelley may cheat himself with the imagined loftiness and independence of his theory, and it is easy to invent a thousand sophisms to reconcile his conscience to the impurity of his practice; but this lasts only long enough to lead him on beyond the power of return; he ceases to be the dupe, but with desperate malignity he becomes the deceiver of others. Like the Egyptians of old, the wheels of his chariot are broken, and the path of 'mighty waters' closes in upon him behind, and a still deepening ocean is before him: for a short time are seen his impotent struggles against a resistless power, his blasphemous execrations are heard, his despair but poorly assumes the tone of triumph and defiance, and he calls ineffectually on others to follow him to the same ruin — finally he sinks 'like lead' to the bottom and is forgotten. So it is now in part, so shortly will it be entirely with Mr. Shelley." The reviewer added that if he might withdraw the veil of private life, and show the true character of the author of *The Revolt of Islam*, it would indeed be a disgusting picture which should be disclosed.

That Mary should have regarded all this as "nothing" shows how immured their minds had become to criticism, however biting. The January *Blackwood* contained a review of quite a different nature. Referring to Shelley, the *Blackwood* critic said: —

"It is impossible to read a page of his *Revolt of Islam* without perceiving that in nerve and pith of conception he approaches more nearly to Scott and Byron than any other of their contemporaries." Again, — "We do not hesitate to say, with all due respect for the character of that journal, that Mr. Shelley has been infamously and stupidly treated in the *Quarterly Review*. His reviewer there, whoever he is, does not show himself a man of such lofty principles as to

So you would put in a word with me about Hogg (and Polypheme also — I do not know if you think they are alike but I believe that the gentleman does himself. But I have written a book in defence of entitle him to ride the high horse in company with the author of *The Revolt of Islam*. And when one compares the *vis inertiae* of his motionless prose with the 'eagle-winged raptures' of Mr. Shelley's poetry, one does not think, indeed, of Satan reproving Sin, but one does think — we will say it in plain words and without a figure — of a dunce rating a man of genius. If that critic does not know that Mr. Shelley is a poet, almost in the very highest sense of that mysterious word, then we appeal to all those whom we have enabled to judge for themselves, if he be not unfit to speak of poetry before the people of England."

Having been unable to get any publisher to undertake the risk of printing *The Revolt of Islam*, Shelley had it printed at his own expense and arranged with several publishers to sell it for his account. It proved to be a literary triumph, but was an almost unmitigated financial failure. A single copy of the first edition would now sell for more than the gross receipts for all the copies that were sold.

Shelley had a similar experience with the publication of *Alastor*, as evidenced by his letter to Ollier of August 8, 1817: — "May I trouble you with a commission, and is it in your range of transaction to undertake it? I published some time since a poem called *Alastor*, at Baldwin's; the sale, I believe, was scarcely anything, but as the printer has sent me in his account, I wish to know also how my account stands with the publisher. He had no interest in the work, nor do I know anyone else had. It is scarcely worth while to [do] anything more with it than to procure a business-like reply on the subject of the state of what is to pay or receive. In case this commission is unusual or disagreeable to you for any reason of which I may be ignorant, I beg that you will not scruple to decline it."

Polypheme, have I not?) — You say that you think that he has a good heart, and so do I; but who can be sure of it? He wraps himself up in a triple veil and places, or appears to place, a high wall between himself and his fellows. This want of confidence and frankness must in its natural course be repaid by a kind of mistrust; and that, with his manners which when unrelieved by the presence of half a dozen people, always disgust me — make him as a constant daily-hourly visitor — which he insists upon being with us — absolutely intolerable. I hope when we return we shall be out of the reach of any but his Sunday visits.

Shelley's doctor (not an Italian — they never do any good) has been of service to him and I hope that he will be of more but the bright sun of this blue sky is of more use than a myriad of medicines and a cold day (we have none of them now) casts him back. The rest of us are well — if it is not that I suffer from ill spirits. God knows why, but I have suffered more from them, ten times over, than I ever did before I came to Italy. Evil thoughts will hang about me — but this is only now and then.

Give our loves to the Darling of Aix la Chapelle. She never writes and never will, I dare say, although I have written to her several times; but of course she has more to do than ever. Of an evening she might, as she has before now, gossip a little with me. Our best remembrances to Bessy and our friends that you may chance to see. God knows when we shall see them. If some chances came about it might be in three months, but it will not be so, I promise you; so wait another year and stay till I date again Rome April 1820, and then we may see some glimmering.

It is a long time since we have heard from Venice, but all goes on as badly there with the noble poet [1] as ever, I fear. He is a lost man if he does not escape soon. Allegra is there with a friend [2] of his and ours, and if fortune will so favour us, things shall remain as they are concerning her another year; but I fear we shall be obliged to move — it is a long story and as usual people have behaved ill, but do not mention these things in your letters.

Adio. — The Romans speak better Italian and have softer voices than their

---

[1] Lord Byron.   [2] The Hoppners.

countrymen. Keep yourself well and walk
out every day — we do.

Affectionately yours,

Mary W. S.

Leghorn, June 29th, 1819

My dear Marianne —

Although we have not heard from you
or of you for some time I hope you are
going on well — that you enjoy our health
and see your children lively about you.

You see by our hap [1] how blind we
mortals are when we go seeking after what
we think our good. We came to Italy
thinking to do Shelley's health good, but
the climate is not [by] any means warm
enough to be of benefit to him, and yet it
is that that has destroyed my two children.
We went from England comparatively
prosperous and happy; I should return
broken hearted and miserable. I never
know one moment's ease from the wretched-
ness and despair that possesses me. May
you, my dear Marianne, never know what
it is to lose two only and lovely children

[1] This refers to the death of their son William, who died
on the 7th of June. On the 12th of the following November
their son Percy was born.

66

in one year — to watch their dying moments, and then at last to be left childless and for ever miserable.

It is useless complaining and I shall therefore only write a short letter, for as all my thoughts are nothing but misery it is not kind to transmit them to you.

Since Shelley wrote to Hunt we have taken a house in the neighbourhood of Leghorn. Be so kind as to inform Peacock of this — and that he must direct us to Ferma in Posta, Livorno and to let us know whether he has sent any letter to Florence. I am very anxious to know whether or not I am to receive the clothes I wrote to you about, for if we do not I must provide others; and although that will be a great expense and trouble yet it would be better for me to know as soon as possible if any one can or will send them. Peacock seems too much taken up in his new occupations to think about us and he unfortunately is the only person who I can have the slightest hope would do such a thing. If you would write to let me know whether you have them or indeed what you know about them, it would exceedingly oblige me; but I know that your domestic concerns leave you no time, therefore I do not expect that you can do me this favour. I wish I had brought them with me; but one can only learn by experience how slowly and badly every thing is done for the absent. Do not think that I reproach you by these words — I know that you can do nothing, and who else is there that would care for my convenience or inconvenience.

I am sorry to write to you all about these petty affairs, but if I would write any-thing else about myself it would only be a list of hours spent in tears and grief. Hunt used to call me serious; what would he say to me now! I feel that I am not fit for anything and therefore not fit to live. But how must that heart be moulded which would not be broken by what I have suffered! William was so good, so beauti-ful, so entirely attached to me! To the last moment almost he was in such abound-ing health and spirits, and his malady appeared of so slight a nature — arising simply from worms, — inspired no fear of danger — that the blow was as sudden as it was terrible. Did you ever know a child with a fine colour, wonderful spirits

— breeding worms (and those of the most innocent kind) that would kill him in a fortnight! We had a most excellent English surgeon to attend him and he allowed that these were the fruits of this hateful Italy.

But all this is all nothing to anyone but myself, and I wish that I were incapable of feeling that or any other sorrow. Give my love to Hunt; keep yourselves well and happy.

Yours,
M. W. SHELLEY

If the child's things are not sent at least as soon as this letter arrives they will come too late; but if I had the hopes that any one would take the trouble to send them at last, I would only make up the things perfectly necessary, in expectation of the others.

Leghorn, 28th August, 1819

My dear Marianne —

We are very dull at Leghorn, and I can therefore write nothing to amuse you. We live in a little country house at the end of a green lane, surrounded by a *podere*. These *poderi* are just the things Hunt would like. They are like our kitchen-gardens, with the difference only that the beautiful fertility of the country gives them. A large bed of cabbages is very unpicturesque in England, but here the furrows are alternated with rows of grapes festooned on their supports, and the hedges are of myrtle, which have just ceased to flower; their flower has the sweetest faint smell in the world, like some delicious spice. Green grassy walks lead you through the vines. The people are always busy, and it is pleasant to see three or four of them transform in one day a bed of Indian corn to one of celery. They work this hot weather in their shirts, or smock-frocks (but their breasts are bare), their brown legs nearly the colour, only with a rich tinge of red in it, of the earth they turn up. They sing, not very melodiously, but very loud, Rossini's music, "Mi rivedrai, ti rivedro," and they are accompanied by the *cicala*, a kind of little beetle, that makes a noise with its tail as loud as Johnny can sing; they live on trees; and three or four together are enough to deafen you. It is to the *cicala* that Anacreon has addressed an ode which they call "To a Grasshopper" in the English translations.

Well, here we live. I never am in good spirits — often in very bad; and Hunt's portrait has already seen me shed so many tears that, if it had his heart as well as his eyes, he would weep too in pity. But no more of this, or a tear will come now, and there is no use for that.

By the bye, a hint Hunt gave about portraits. The Italian painters are very bad; they might make a nose like Shelley's, and perhaps a mouth, but I doubt it; but there would be no expression about it. They have no notion of anything except copying again and again their Old Masters; and somehow mere copying, however divine the original, does a great deal more harm than good.

Shelley has written a good deal, and I have done very little since I have been in Italy. I have had so much to see, and so many vexations, independently of those which God has kindly sent to wean me from the world if I were too fond of it. Shelley has not had good health by any means, and, when getting better, fate has ever contrived something to pull him back. He never was better than the last month of his stay in Rome, except the last week —

then he watched sixty miserable death-like hours without closing his eyes; [1] and you may think what good that did him.

We see the *Examiners* regularly now, four together, just two months after the publication of the last. These are very delightful to us. I have a word to say to Hunt of what he says concerning Italian dancing. The Italians dance very badly. They dress for their dances in the ugliest manner; the men in little doublets, with a hat and feather; they are very stiff; nothing but their legs move; and they twirl and jump with as little grace as may be. It is not for their dancing, but their pantomime, that the Italians are famous. You remember what we told you of the ballet of *Othello*. They tell a story by action, so that words appear perfectly superfluous things for them. In that they are graceful, agile, impressive, and very affecting; so that I delight in nothing so much as a deep tragic ballet. But the dancing, unless, as they sometimes do, they dance as common people (for instance, the dance of joy of the Venetian citizens

[1] Shelley spent these anxious, wakeful hours beside the sick bed of their little William.

on the return of Othello), is very bad indeed.

I am very much obliged to you for all your kind offers and wishes. Hunt would do Shelley a great deal of good, but that we may not think of; his spirits are tolerably good. But you do not tell me how you get on; how Bessy is, and where she is. Remember me to her. Clare is learning thorough bass and singing. We pay four crowns a month for her master, lessons three times a week; cheap work this, is it not? At Rome we paid three shillings a lesson and the master stayed two hours. The one we have now is the best in Leghorn.

I write in the morning, read Latin till two, when we dine; then I read some English book, and two cantos of Dante with Shelley. In the evening our friends the Gisbornes come, so we are not perfectly alone. I like Mrs. Gisborne very much indeed, but her husband is most dreadfully dull; and as he is always with her, we have not so much pleasure in her company as we otherwise should. . . .

73

Leghorn, Sept. 24th, 1819

My dear Hunt —

How very thankful we are to you for your Monday letters. This is truly kind of you, and yet we have both been very ungrateful, and not answered them as we ought. For me I hardly need make any excuse, for I am so seldom in a humour when any letter of mine could be in any degree amusing or acceptable; and Shelley has for the last days been so occupied with our friends here from various causes — that with that, and his poem which you will have received — and his Spanish — for Clare's brother has been here — he has passed fifteen months in Spain — and Shelley having made some progress in Spanish before he came he wished to take advantage of his short stay here to improve himself more — with all these things his time has been fully taken up. Yesterday he went to Florence to take lodgings for us. I shall be confined there some time next month, and we shall probably spend the whole winter there — somewhat dully to be sure, since we shall not know a soul there; and there is little to amuse us in looking at one another and reading there

74

what we already too well know. Yet I am the worst at this, for latterly Shelley's spirits have been tolerably good and his health much improved, although the variableness of this climate is not very good for him. The transitions from heat to cold are worse here than in England: for instance, three days ago we had the finest weather in the world — so hot that you could not stir out in the middle of the day, and now it has become as cold as sometimes I have felt it at Christmas in England. This will not last, for when the wind changes it will become warm again. In the mean time we freeze in an Italian-built house that lets in the wind on every side — no fire-places, and stone floors. The Italians although having so much hotter weather than we, and feeling the heat more than we — yet are not nearly so sensible to the cold as us, and take very few precautions against the cold season except holding a little earthenware pot with charcoal in it in their hands.

In my last letter I answered your kind words about pictures. Italian artists cannot make portraits. We may chance to find an English or German at Florence, and if so I will persuade Shelley to sit. As for me it would have been very well six months ago, but now I could not persuade myself to sit to be painted. I can assure you I am much changed. The world will never be to me again as it was; there was a life and freshness in it that is lost to me. On my last birthday when I was twenty-one I repined that time should fly so quickly and that I should grow older so quickly. This birthday — now I am twenty-two — although the time since the last seems to have flown with speed of lightning, yet I rejoiced at that and only repined that I was not older; in fact I ought to have died on the 7th of June last.

I am very much obliged to Marianne for the trouble she has taken about my commissions. Of course the parcel has been sent long ago. In your next letter I hope to have the bill of lading or at least the name of the Captain and vessel, and then it will entirely depend on whether the vessel quits London directly. I am very anxious for some of the things.

It gives me great pleasure to hear that you have such good hopes of Thornton.

Pray how does Johnny get on, and have you now another? How very happy you must feel amidst all their noise and bother, when you think of our desolate situation. Marianne might well laugh, if it were a laughing matter, at the recollection of my preachments about having so large a family, when I now say that I wish I had a dozen — any thing but none, or one — a fearful risk on whom all one's hopes and joy is placed! Why do I write about this! Why, because I can write of nothing else, and that is why I write so seldom.

My best and most affectionate wishes are with you. Take care of yourselves and pray write still every week. Clare sends her love — to Bessy also. Is she still with her brother? Pray tell us.

Yours ever,

Mary W. Shelley

I must say a word of Mr. Gisborne whom you will see. You will find him a very dull man, but if you take any trouble about him you will be well repaid when Mrs. G. joins him, for she is an excellent woman; and, what you will think praise, very much attached to Shelley; to me too perhaps, but I am nothing now and it is impossible any one can much like so dull a person.

As you talked of moving at Michaelmas I direct this letter to the *E[xaminer]* office. A letter was sent yesterday with a poem in it, directed to York Buildings.

Florence, Nov. 24th, 1819

My dear Marianne —

At length I am afraid Hunt has got tired of his Monday remembrances. I cannot tell you how this vexes me; perhaps he thinks that my little Percy will serve instead; but why not have two pleasant things instead of one? Ask him to be very good, and to continue his practice, which was the pleasantest in the world. Tell him we have few friends in any part of Italy — none in Florence — and none whom we love as well as we love him: make him always consider it a *Black Monday* when he does not write a little to us.

A few days before we left Leghorn, which is now two months ago, Shelley sent a poem called the Mask of Anarchy. Hunt does not mention the reception of it — it was directed to York buildings, and he is anxious to know whether it has been received. You will have received several other large packets from him. You will ask Ollier for money to pay for these extra extraordinary letters; but just let us hear of their safe arrival. We have to thank Bessy for her kindness in transscribing Hunt's kindness, but it so happened that the practical Peacock had thought it worth while to send those three *Examiners* themselves to us by post. Pray how is the said gentleman going on? He is not yet married and says he does not think about it. I am afraid *his* Marianne does, and somewhat bitterly. She had rather, perhaps, that he were still faithfully rusticating at Marlow; for this shepherd-King has, I am afraid, forgotten his crook and his mistress. Do not show him this gossip of mine concerning him on any account.

After writing this long page I need not tell you that I am very well, and the little boy [1] also. He was born a small child, but has grown so during this first fortnight that if his little face were not always the same one might almost think him a changed child. He takes after me. You see I

[1] Her son, Percy.

say more about him than Hunt did of his little Harry, but he is my only one and although he is so healthy and promising that for the life of me I cannot fear, yet it is a bitter thought that all should be risked on one. Yet how much sweeter than to be childless, as I was for five hateful months! Do not let us talk of those five months: when I look back on all I suffered at Leghorn I shudder with horror; yet even now a sickening feeling steps in the way of every enjoyment when I think — of what I will not write about.

I hope all your children are well. They must all be grown quite out of our knowledge. Years can hardly give steadiness to Thornton, and Johnny and Mary are yet in the jumping age. Give them a kiss, they and the three younger ones, including the little stranger.

You have no notion how many admirers Hunt has got here by means of his picture, especially among our lady acquaintances (English). I had corked up in my memory a number of soft and tender exclamations concerning his eyes and his hair and his forehead, etc. I have forgotten them, unfortunately, but really from the effect his phisiognomy produces on all who see him and the warmth with which people defend him after seeing it — who were cool before, and their vows that indeed he cannot be the Bristol Hunt, I should think that his friends ought to club to have his picture painted by Owen or Lawrence and exhibited, and then no one would think ill of him more.

Shelley in his last letter mentioned something about his return to England, but this is very vague. I hope — how ardently you may guess — that it will not be; but in any case keep it quite a secret, as if he came, hardly a creature must know it. We have been pursued by so much ill luck that I cannot hope, and dare not, that things will turn out well. But his return would be in so many ways so dreadful a thing that I cannot dwell long enough upon the idea as to conceive it possible. We do not think of all returning. Since we have returned to Tuscany we have lived for the first time in an economical manner, and it would be madness to break this up; besides that, arrests and a thousand other things render it impossible that we should be known to be in England.

(November 25th). Another post day and no letter from any of you, who I must tell you are the only people from whom we receive any letters except concerning business. Peacock's correspondence having degenerated since the time he had nought to do but to tune his pipe in Bisham wood.

I could ask a thousand questions about you and yours, but I am afraid that they would not be answered, and so instead I will talk to you of ourselves. You may judge by what Shelley has sent to England that he has been very busily employed; and besides this he often spends many hours of the day at the Gallery admiring and studying the statues and pictures. There are many divine ones, he says; for my part I have not seen anything except one peep I took at the Venus di Medici, which is not a striking statue — both from its size and the meaningless expression of the countenance; the form requires study to understand its full merit.

Clare has got now a very good singing master and is getting on exceedingly well. Tell Hunt that there is a beautiful song —

Non temete, O Madre Amata — of Azzioli's — only a few copies of which were printed. I wish he could get it to sing to me when I return. When will that be? I must answer with the nursery rhyme, — When I grow rich.

After having heard that the box you so kindly sent was shipped from Genoa we have heard no more of it. Fortunately a box from Peacock contained the things I so indispensably needed, but I am now in great want of the flannel for the child.

I long to hear from you. I wish you could squeeze a hour for a letter. Love from all to all. Have you received Peter Bell Third, etc.?

Yours affectionately and entirely,
MARY W. SHELLEY

We have at last received Bessy's letter, my dear Marianne, when the long protracted silence of our poor dear friend made us fear that he must be engaged in some plot or other with T—d or others, so to engross his time that for three months (and during cold weather too) he could not send one look to Italy. But it appears that he is only engaged in the same plot that exercises all the world, viz., *care;* and I would write a great deal to say how melancholy it makes me to see all my friends oppressed by the same load. But I wish letters from Italy to be a recreation and to draw you out of your cares as much as vain words and kind remembrances can. Although before I leave the subject of your *cares*, my dear, let me advert to your *health*. Bessy says in her letter that Percy, from a sickly infant is grown a fine stout boy; he appears to have been in the same case as Swinburne, and I am afraid from the same cause. I could say a great many things to prove to you that a woman is not a field to be continually employed either in bringing forth or enlarging grain, but I say only take care of yourself and so I pass on to something else.

We are now comfortably settled in Pisa for three months more than we have already staid, and then we go again to the Baths of Lucca. Shelley's health is so very delicate that little as he can bear cold, heat is almost more injurious to him and he is ordered to seek the coolest climate Tuscany affords, i.e., the Baths of Lucca:

84

besides, the Baths themselves are recommended for him. The most famous surgeon in all Italy lives at Pisa — Vacca. He is a very pleasant man, a great republican, and no Xtian. He tells Shelley to take care of himself and strengthen himself, but to take no medicine. At Pisa we have an apartment on the Lung' Arno, a street that runs the length of the town on each side of the Arno, and the side which receives the southern sun is the warmest and freshest climate in the world. We have two bedrooms, two sittingrooms, kitchen, servants rooms nicely furnished, and very clean and *new* — a great thing in this country — for four guineas and a half a month. The rooms are light and airy, so you see we begin to profit by Italian prices. One learns this very slowly, but I assure you a crown here goes as far in the conveniences and necessaries of life as one pound in England and if it were not for claims on us and expenses that are as it were external, or perhaps rather internal, for they belong to ourselves and not to the country we live in, we should be very rich indeed. As it is, for the first time in our lives we get on easily, our minds undisturbed by weekly bills and daily expenses, and with a little care we expect to get the things into better order than they are.

Only one thing teazes us: Elise has married, and Milly has quitted us, and we have only Italian servants who teaze us out of our lives. I am trying to get a Swiss, and hope that I shall succeed. We see no society, it is true, except one or two English who are friends and not acquaintances. We might if we pleased, but it is so much trouble to begin, and I am so much confined and my time is so much taken up with my child that I should grudge the time. However, in the summer or next winter we shall, I think, mix a little with the Italians. Pisa is a pretty town, but its inhabitants would exercise all Hogg's vocabulary of scamps, raffs, etc., etc., to fully describe their ragged-haired, shirtless condition. Many of them are students of the university and they are none of the genteelest of the crew. Then there are *Bargees*, beggars without number; galley slaves in their yellow and red dress with chains, the women in dirty cotton gowns trailing in the dirt, pink silk hats starting *up* in the air to run away from their ugly faces in this manner:

for they always tie the bows at the points [of] their chins — and white satin shoes, and fellows with bushy hair, large whiskers, canes in their hands, and a bit of dirty party coloured ribband (symbol of nobility) sticking in their buttonholes — that mean to look like the lords of the rabble, but who only look like their drivers. The Pisans I dislike more than any of the Italians, and none of them are as yet favourites with me. Not that I much wish to be in England, if I could but import a cargo of friends and books from that island here. I am too much depressed by its enslaved state, my inutility; the little chance there is for freedom, and the great chance there is for tyranny, to wish to be witness of its degradation step by step, and to feel all the sensations of indignation and horror which I know I should experience were I to hear daily the talk of the subjects, or rather the slaves, of King Cant whose dominion I fear is of wider extent in England than anywhere else. At present I have it double distilled through Galignani, and even thus frittered way it makes one almost sick. No; since I have seen Rome, that City is my Country, and I do not wish to own any other until England is *free* and *true;* that is, until the throne *Cant,* the God, or if you will, the abominable idol, before whom at present the English are offering up a sacrifice of blood and liberty, be overthrown. Cant has more power in Parliament, and over the kingdom than fear or any other motive. A man now in England would as soon think of refusing a duel as of not listening to and talking the language of *Cant,* and from the same motive he would be afraid of being turned out of society.

Besides these reasons you know many others, my dear Marianne, of an individual nature that keep us from returning. If we had no debts yet they would instantly accumulate if we went back to England; and then Shelley's health — the more we see and hear the more we are convinced

88

that this climate is absolutely necessary
to him. Not that this is a Paradise of
cloudless skies and windless air — just now
the *Il Vecchio* is blowing hurricanes, but
they are equinoctial gales — but it's so
much better than your northern island.
But do not think that I am un-Englishifying
myself, but that nook of *ci-devant* free
land, so sweetly surrounded by the sea is
no longer England, but Castlereagh land
or New Land Castlereagh. Heaven defend
me from being a Castlereaghish woman!
What say you to Hunt's gravely putting
a letter in his *Examiner* as from a cor-
respondent saying that on the approaching
election and during the present state of the
country it is dangerous to repeat the name
of England, which has become the watch-
word of rebellion [1] and irreligion, and that
while the land continues in its present
demoralized and disturbed state all loyal
persons should distinguish themselves by
assuming for their country the denomina-
tion I before mentioned? The more loyal
one, which would be Georgia, is objection-

[1] The Manchester Massacre of August 16, 1819, and
attacks on the liberty of the press moved Shelley to write
The Mask of Anarchy.

able on account of the immorality of the women of the region that goes by that name; which by association might have a bad effect on the imaginations of our chaste country women of unblemished reputation!!!! Is not this the talk of God Cant? and of his prime council the Exxxxxh Parliament? And of his prime organ the *Courier* newspaper? But I really think an excellent plan might be made of it. All those who wish to become subjects of the new kingdom ought to be obliged to take an oath of citizenship, not as Irish, English or Scotch, but as Castlereaghish. All that refused should be put on the Alien list; besides the Government should have the right to refuse subjects — what a picnic kingdom it would become! One of the first things would be to import a cargo of subjects from all various oppressed countries on the earth; not to free them, but as good examples for the rest. A man would only have to enter himself a slave, a fool, a bigot and a tyrant where he can, to become a Castlereaghishman. The form of their oath should be, — The King shall have my breath, Castlereagh my obedience, his Parliament my love, the *Courier* my trust, the *Quarterly* my belief, Murray my custom — down with the Whigs and Radicals — So God help me! Their belief may be easily exprest: "I believe in Cant, the creator of this kingdom, the supporter of Castlereagh, and maker of all fortunes, the sole rule of life, and the life of all morality — created by fear, falsehood and hate; brought into fashion by Castlereagh, for the use of Castlereaghish men and women — detested by the Whigs, yet used by them; detested by the Radicals whom it detests; born long ago, but grew much since the French Revolution, and more since the establishment of the most holy Kingdom New Land Castlereagh — may it never die! As it has changed all truth to a lie, so does it live in and by lies, and may its food never fail; nor can it while we exist! I believe in all that Cant teaches, as it is revealed to me by the *Courier* and the *Quarterly*, and sold to me by Murray, whom Cant bless. I believe in all plots Cant feigns and creates, and will use none but the language of Cant unto my last day — amen!"

I really think I will write to Castlereagh on the subject; it would be a Godsend to

him, such a kingdom, and save him a
world of trouble in grinding and pounding
and hanging and taxing the English that
remain, into Castlereaghish, for all that
would not accede to the terms of his agree-
ment would be aliens and so an end to
them. You see what a John, or rather
Joan Bull I am, so full of politics. But I
entreat you to adopt my vocabulary and
call all that can support so vile a wretch
as that detested Irishman by their proper
name. Do not degrade the name of British;
they are and ever must be Castlereaghish
— which pronounced in a short way Castle-
raish wont be very uncouth and will be
very apt.

I hope that we shall soon hear of your
health and well-being, my dear Marianne.
Little Percy has got the measles very
lightly. It is a much milder malady in
this climate than with you, and he has got
it mildly for this climate. Do pray you
or Hunt write. Bessy's letter is dated the
6th January, so God knows what may
have happened since then — nothing ill
I trust. But we now begin to feel that we
are not travellers, but exiles — since our
English friends neglect and forget us.

92

What say you to this reproach? Or will
you consider it as one?

Adieu, dear Marianne.

Affectionately yours ever,

MARINA W. S.

Pisa (direct to us here).

Feb. 24th, 1820

We have just received Hunt's letter.
It is dreadful to see how much he is teased.
I hope sincerely that you are now going on
better. Do you write — Does he think I
could write for his *Indicator*, and what kind
of thing would he like? Shelley will answer his letter next week. Adieu.

Pisa, 3rd December, 1820.

Do you think, dear friend, that we are
very pleased to write thousands and thousands of letters and to receive no reply?
You are cruel! Why? Indeed I can hardly
keep account of the days, the long weeks
and the still longer months that have
passed while none of them brings us your
letters. Mariana and you are equally un-
faithful. Who knows what may have
become of you? Perhaps a Laplandish
witch has carried you, not to the soft air

93

and the delightful countries of the South, but to some horrid frozen and hateful land which has frozen all your love for us. I certainly think, however, that you in England are harder and harsher than we, when I see that so few of all the nobles defended the unfortunate Queen, whom I really think is most innocent. I have great pity for this woman and when one considers the great difference between the villainous King and this pious and good Queen, who goes to visit a servant struck down by the plague, one gets furious. He, whose character you have yourself portrayed so well, as one of the worst, and she, whose greatest fault is to enjoy herself amongst her servants instead of staying alone by herself, when entirely abandoned by the slavish grandees of England. It is well known that the feeling against her which exists in Italy was aroused by the spies. Notwithstanding this strong feeling, however, all Italians say that the evidence was certainly not sufficient for condemning her and, in truth, it seems to me that they have now, after the trial, a much more favourable opinion of her than previously. Everyone has been horrified by the indecency of this ever infamous trial.

In the meantime we received a letter from dear Mariana who tells us that you would write a letter to us; but up to the present, this letter so much looked forward to has not arrived.

I must tell you, dear friend, of a professor [1] with whom we have become acquainted in Pisa. He is really the only Italian who has a heart and soul. He is very high spirited, has a profound mind and an eloquence which enraptures. The poor people of Pisa think him mad and they tell many little stories about him, which make us believe that he is really somewhat extravagant or, as the English say, "eccentric." He, however, says, "They think I am mad and it gives me pleasure that they should be deceiving themselves in that way; the time, however, may perhaps come when they will see that it is the madness of Brutus." Every evening he comes to our house and always delights us with his original ideas.

[1] This was Professor Pacchiani, "who," says Mrs. Marshall, "had been, if he was not still, a university professor, but who was none the less an adventurer and an impostor. . . . He amused but did not please the Shelleys."

He speaks the Italian language beautifully, quite different from the present idiom, so that we receive the impression of listening to Boccaccio or Machiavelli, as he speaks as they have written.

We have further made the acquaintance of an Improvisor,[1] a man of great talent, very well up in Greek and of an incomparable poetic mind. He improvises with admirable fervour and justice. His subject was the future destiny of Italy; he recalled to mind that Petrarch said that neither the highest Alps nor the sea were sufficient to defend this vacillating and ancient country from foreign masters; but he said, "I see the Alps growing higher and even the sea rising and becoming troubled so as to keep off its enemies." Unfortunately, he also, as some poets of our country, finds greater pleasure in the momentary applause of a theatre and in the admiration of women, than in studying for posterity.

You see that in the meantime we get to know a little more every day of the Italians and we take a very lively interest in the war threatening Naples — what will they do? The nobles of Naples are indepen-

[1] This was Sgricci, the celebrated Improvvisatore.

dent and brave, but the people are slaves, —
who knows whether the militia will be
able to resist the Austrian arms!

All the Italians, without exception, sigh
for liberty; but, as in every country, the
poor have no power and the wealthy ones
do not wish to risk their money. The
Italians love money perhaps more than
the English. The wealthy classes in England love gold, but the nobles of Italy are
fond of copper and small coin. The quat-
trini (half farthings) are considered by
them as much as the shillings by us. There
is another acquaintance of ours, romantic
and pathetic, a young girl [1] of nineteen
years of age, the daughter of a Florentine
noble; very beautiful, very talented, who
writes Italian with an elegance and delicacy
equal to the foremost authors of the best
Italian epoch. She is, however, most unhappy. Her mother is a very bad woman;
and, as she is jealous of the talents and
beauty of her daughter, she shuts her up
in a convent where she sees nothing else
but the servants and idiots. She never

[1] The girl here referred to was the beautiful Emilia
Viviani, to whom Shelley dedicated *Epipsycbidion*, and on
whom he had what in modern parlance would be called a
crusb; but it was of short duration and did no violence.

goes out, but is shut up in two small rooms which look out on the not very picturesque kitchen garden of the convent. She always laments her pitiful condition. Her only hope is to get married, but even her existence is nearly a secret, and what marriage will it be? I will tell you, dear friend, how they marry in this country. I can assure you of the truth of this because, while I am writing, I have before my eyes a demand in marriage of a girl of Pisa. The advocate who is employed to make this proposal sends a letter which commences as follows: "The young man with whom it is desired to join in marriage the girl in question is in his 17th year. He is tall and well-built, without any imperfection, in the best of health, strong and good looking, he is of good moral character and his knowledge is unsurpassed; he is studious and sufficiently advanced in the study of the fine arts to which he earnestly devotes himself." Then follows a description of his family and of his fortune and expectations and of the dowry which he expects, and this masterpiece finishes as follows: "The marriage will have to be celebrated two years after the making of this contract. When the parents of the intended bride shall have approved the above conditions the name of the young man in question will be immediately made known. Finally, it is necessary to know the age of the intended bride." This is an Italian marriage. Moreover, they have a great horror of marriages which are concluded without the consent of the parents. Certainly domestic tyranny has greater power here in the minds of people as well as in law; notwithstanding this, the parents, with few exceptions, are tender and indulgent in every day life.

Up to the present we have not had any winter. We enjoy mild air and beautiful sunshine in December; the autumn rains have not come to pass and the country, although bare and leafless, looks pleasant under the brightness of the very clear sky. Dear friend, leave your troubles behind and enjoy for a few minutes also my beautiful Italy. I hope that this letter will have the desired effect. May God preserve you and all yours. Shelley and Chiarina send many thousands of affectionate greetings. Goodbye.

Your constant friend,

MARINA

December 29, 1820

My dear friend —

We have been very anxious to hear from you since we saw that your paper had been honoured with the peculiar attention of the H.G. Yet no letters come. I am convinced that you will escape when it comes to trial, but an acquittal must be bought not only with anxiety, fear and labour, but also with the money you can so ill spare. Before this comes to hand you will of course have written — one of your letters which are as rare as Fountains in the Stony Arabia will have given us a brief pleasure. Why do you not write oftener? Ah! why are you not rich, peaceful and enjoying? We have just been delighted with a parcel of your *Indicators*, but they also afford full proof that you are not as happy as you ought to be. Yet how beautiful they are! That one upon the deaths of young children was a piece of as fine writing and of as exquisite feeling as I ever read. To us you know it must have been particularly affecting. Yet there is one thing well apparent — you, my dear Hunt, never lost a child or the ideal immortality would not suffice to your imagination as it naturally does, thinking only of those whom you loved more from the over-flowing of affection than from their being the hope, the rest, the purpose, the support, and the recompense of life. I hardly know whether I do not teaze you with too many letters, yet you have made no complaint of that, and besides you always like to hear about the Italians, and it is almost impossible not to write something pleasing to you from this divine country, if praises of its many beauties and its delights be interesting to you. I have now an account to give you of a wonderful and beautiful exhibition of talent which we have been witnesses of; an exhibition peculiar to the Italians and like their climate, their vegetation and their country, fervent, fertile and mixing in wondrous proportions the picturesque, the cultivated and the wild until they become, not as in other countries, one the foil of the other, but they mingle and form a spectacle new and beautiful. We were the other night at the theatre where the Improvvisatore whom I mentioned in my last letter delivered an extempore tragedy. Conceive of a poem as long as a Greek

Tragedy, interspersed with choruses, the whole plan conceived in an instant. The ideas and verses and scenes flowing in rich succession like the perpetual gush of a fast falling cataract. The ideas poetic and just; the words the most beautiful, *scette* and grand that his exquisite Italian afforded. He is handsome; his person small but elegant, and his motions graceful beyond description: his action was perfect; and the freedom of his motions outdo the constraint which is ever visible in an English actor. The changes of countenance were of course not so fine as those I have witnessed on the English stage, for he had not conned his part and set his features, but it was one impulse that filled him; an unchanged deity who spoke within him, and his voice surpassed in its modulations the melody of music. The subject was Iphigenia in Tauris. It was composed on the Greek plan (indeed he followed Euripides in his arrangement and in many of his ideas) without the division of acts and with choruses. Of course if we saw it written there would have been many slight defects of management — defects amended when seen, but many of the scenes were perfect; and the recognition of Orestes and Iphigenia was worked up beautifully.

I do not know how this talent may be appreciated in the other cities of Italy, but the Pisans are noted for their want of love, and of course entire ignorance of the fine arts. Their opera is miserable, their theatre the worst in Italy. The theatre was nearly empty on this occasion. The students of the University half filled the pit and the few people in the boxes were foreigners, except two Pisan families who went away before it was half over. God knows what this man would be if he laboured and became a poet for posterity instead of an Improvvisatore for the present. I am enclined to think that in the perfection in which he possesses this art it is by no means an inferior power to that of a *printed poet*. There have been few Improvvisatores who have, like him, joined a cultivated education and acquirements in languages rare among foreigners. If, however, his auditors were refined — and as the oak or the rock to the lightning — feeling in their inmost souls the penetrative fire of his poetry — I should not find fault with his making perfection in this art the aim of his exertions. But to improvise to a Pisan audience is to scatter otto of roses among the overweighing stench of a charnel house: pearls to swine were economy in comparison. As Shelley told him the other night, he appeared in Pisa as Dante among the ghosts. Pisa is a city of the dead and they shrunk from his living presence. The name of this Improvvisatore is Sgricci, and I see that his name is mentioned in your literary pocket book. This has made me think that it were an interesting plan for this same pretty pocket book if you were to give some small interesting account — not exactly a biographical sketch, but *anecdotical* and somewhat critical of the various authors of the list. Sgricci has been accused of carbonarism, whether truly or not I cannot judge. I should think not or he would be trying to harvest at Naples instead of extemporizing here. From what we have heard of him I believe him to be good, and his manners are gentle and amiable; while the rich flow of his beautifully pronounced language is as pleasant to the ear as a sonata of Mozart. I must tell you that some wiseacre Professors of

Pisa wanted to put Sgricci down at the theatre and their vile envy might have frightened the God from his temple if an Irishman who chanced to be in the same box with them had not compelled them to silence. The ringleader of this gang is called Rossini — a man, a speaker of folly in a city of fools bad, envious, talkative, presumptuous; one "chi mai parla bene di chichesisia — o di quei che vivono o dei morti." He has written a long poem which no one has ever read, and like the illustrious Sotherby, gives the law to a few distinguished Blues of Pisa. Well, good night; tomorrow I will finish my letter and talk to you about our unfortunate young friend, Emilia Viviani.

It is grievous to see this beautiful girl wearing out the best years of her life in an odious convent where both mind and body are sick from want of the appropriate exercise of each. I think she has great talent, if not genius — or if not an internal fountain how could she have acquired the mastery she has of her own language which she writes so beautifully or those ideas which lift her so far above the rest of the Italians. She has not studied much and now hopeless from a five years' confinement everything disgusts her and she looks with hatred and distaste even on the alleviations of her situation. Her only hope is in a marriage, which her parents tell her is concluded, although she has never seen the person intended for her, nor do I think the change of situation will be much for the better, for he is a younger brother and will live in the house with his mother, who they say is *motta sceante.* Yet she may then have the free use of her limbs; she may then be able to walk out among the fields, vineyards and woods of her country and see the mountains and the sky and not be, as now, a dozen steps to the right and then back to the left another dozen, which is the longest walk her convent garden affords; and that, you may be sure, she is very seldom tempted to take.

Winter began with us on Xmas day — not that we have yet had frost, but a cold wind sweeps over us and the sky is covered with dark clouds and the cold sleet mizzles down. I understand that you have had as yet a mild winter. This and the plentiful harvest will keep the poor somewhat happier this year; yet I dare say you now see the white snow before your doors. Even warm as we are here Shelley suffers a great deal of pain in every way — perhaps more even than last winter.

(Jan. 1, 1821). — Although I almost think it of bad augury to wish you a good new year, yet as I finish my letter on this day I cannot help adding the Compliments of the Season and wishing all happiness, peace and enjoyment for this coming year to you my dear dear Marianne — and all who belong to you. I thank you for all the good wishes I know you have made for us. We are quiet now; last year there were many turbulences; perhaps during this there will be fewer.

We have made acquaintance with a Greek, a Prince Mavro Codarti [1] — a very pleasant man profound in his own language and who although he has applied to English little more than a month, begins to relish its beauties, to understand the genius of its expressions in a wonderful manner.

[1] She probably refers to Prince Mavrocordato, to whom at a somewhat later date Shelley dedicated his *Hellas.* Two years after Shelley's death Trelawny wrote to Mary: "A word as to your wooden god, Mavrocordato. . . . I hope, ere long to see his head removed from his worthless body. He is a mere shuffling soldier, an aristocratic brute."

He was done up by some alliance, I believe, with Ali Pacha and has taken refuge in Italy from the Constantinopolitan bowstring. He has related to us some very infamous conduct of the English powers in Greece, of which I should exceedingly like to get the documents to place them in Grey Bennett's or Sir F. B.'s hands. They might serve to give another knock to this wretched system of things.

We are very anxious to hear the event of the meeting of Parliament, as I suppose you all are in England; but perhaps we exiles are ultra-political. But certainly I have some hopes that something fortunate will soon happen for the state of things in England.

And Italy! the King of Naples has gone to Trophau with consent of his Parliament, and that is the latest news. We begin, we hope, to see the crimson clouds of rising peace; and if all is quiet southward we have some thoughts of emigrating there next summer.

Adieu, my dear Hunt.

Most affectionately yours,

MARINA

The foregoing letter, so far as appears, is Mary's last to the Hunts prior to the death of Shelley on July 8, 1822, at which time the Hunts were also in Italy. Shelley's last lines were penned in a poem welcoming Hunt there. From the date of this letter to the time of Shelley's death Mary appears to have been too much occupied in literary work to give much time to letter writing. On August 4, 1821, she wrote in her journal —"Shelley's Birthday. Seven years are now gone; what changes! What a life! We now appear tranquil, yet who knows what wind — but I will not prognosticate evil; we have had enough of it."

Who knew, indeed, what was in store for poor Mary — that her Shelley was to be lost in less than a year! The next winter following his death, Mary spent with the Hunts in Genoa.

After Shelley's death Mary's scattering letters to her various friends were extremely melancholy. Indeed he formed so great a part of her life that his loss seemed to deprive her of all her faculties, except those of intense mental anguish. She was so stunned that for months she moved about like an automaton, scarcely heedful of her surroundings, yet suffering the keenest tortures that human mentality is capable of enduring. She was as incapable of being consoled by others as a dead tree in the forest is incapable of recovering its splendour from the foliage of those about it. With Shelley all her philosophy and courage perished, and for a considerable time she was utterly powerless to recover them. Three months after Shelley's death she wrote in her journal —

"The date still remains — the fatal 8th — a monument to show that all ended then. And I begin again? Oh, never! But several motives induce me, when the day has gone down, and all is silent around me, to pen, as occasion wills, my reflections and feelings. First, I have no friend. For eight years I communicated, with unlimited freedom, with one whose genius, far transcending mine, awakened and guided my thoughts. . . . Now I am alone, — oh, how alone! The stars may behold my tears and the wind drink my sighs, but my thoughts are a sealed treasure which I confide to none."

Again, three days later she wrote —

"I would endeavour to consider myself

a faint continuation of his being, and, as far as possible, the revelation to the earth of what he was; yet, to become this, I must change much, and, above all, I must acquire that knowledge and drink at those fountains of wisdom and virtue from which he quenched his thirst. Hitherto I have done nothing; yet I have not been discontented with myself. I speak of the period of my residence here. For, although unoccupied by those studies which I have marked out for myself, my mind has been so active that its activity, and not its indolence, has made me neglectful. But now the society of others causes this perpetual working of my ideas somewhat to pause; and I must take advantage of this to turn my mind towards its immediate duties, and to determine with firmness to commence the life I have planned. You will be with me in all my studies, dearest love! your voice will no longer applaud me, but in spirit you will visit and encourage me: I know you will. What were I, if I did not believe that you still exist? It is not with you as with another, I believe that we all live hereafter; but you, my only one, were a spirit caged, an elemental being, enshrined in a frail image, now shattered. Do they not all with one voice assert the same? — Trelawny, Hunt, and many others? And so at last you quitted this painful prison, and you are free, my Shelley, while I, your poor chosen one, am left to live as I may."

August 18th, Paris [1823]
My dear Hunt —
I have just returned from spending three days at Versailles. I went to dine and sleep one night, and the Kennys being there, and my dining at their house, made me remain a day longer than I intended. H. S.[1] was very polite, as was also Mrs. S., who in truth is in very delicate health; besides Eliza and Horace they have only one child a little girl two and a half years old, all life and spirits and chattering. Eliza is at home; she seems a nice girl enough, and H. S. seems happy in his domestic circle, pleased with France, which Mrs. S. is not, so they will return to England — God knows when! I was pleased to see the Kennys, especially Kenny, since he is much, dear Hunt, in your circle and

[1] Shelley's friend, Horace Smith.

I asked him accordingly a number of questions. They have an immense family, and a little house quite full; and in the midst of a horde of uninteresting beings, one graceful and amiable creature, Louisa Holcroft,[1] the eldest of Holcroft's girls by Mrs. Kenny. She is now I suppose about two and twenty; she attends to the whole family and her gentleness and sweetness seems the spirit to set all right. I like to see her and Kenny together; they appear so affectionately attached. You would like to see them too — very pretty with bright eyes and animated but unaffected and simple manners; her blushes cover her cheeks whenever she speaks, or whenever mamma is going to tell an unlucky story, which she has vainly endeavoured to interrupt with — "Oh, mamma, not *that!*" Kenny has just brought out an extremely successful opera at the Haymarket. It was to have been played at Drury Lane but "Constantia gone! Amazement!" (I made them laugh by telling them this) refused to act if he did not have Elliston's part, which could not be conceded to him. Poor Kenny is in spirits at the success of

[1] She was a friend of Charles Lamb.

his piece, and is not half so nervous as he was, neither apparently nor really, as Louisa tells me. I have a sort of instinctive liking for these *Authors*, and besides was glad to talk of something with a person of observation after having exhausted my Nothings with Mrs. S. So Louisa, Kenny and I drew together in a corner and talked first of the Godwins and then of the Lambs: I will reverse this order in writing of them to you.

Two years ago the Lambs made an excursion to France. When at Amiens poor Miss L. was taken ill in her usual way, and Lamb was in despair; he met, however, with some acquaintances, who got Miss L. into proper hands and L. came on to Versailles and staid with the Kennys, going on very well, if the French wine had not been too good for him; so I found him no favourite with the S.'s. Poor Miss Lamb is again ill just now. They have been moving, renouncing town and country house to take one which was neither, or either, at Islington, I think they said. Kenny was loud in her praise, saying that he thought her a faultless creature, possessing every virtue under heaven. He was annoyed to find L[amb] more reserved and shut up than usual, avoiding his old friends and not so cordial or amiable as his wont. I asked him about Hazlitt. This love-sick youth, jilted by Infelice, has taken to falling in love. He told Kenny that whereas formerly he thought women silly, unamusing toys, and people with whose society he delighted to dispense, he was now only happy where they were and given up to the admiration of their interesting foibles and amiable weaknesses. He is the humble servant of all marriageable young ladies. Oh! Polly! Wordsworth was in town not long ago, publishing and looking old.

Coleridge is well, having been ill. Procter is ill, and fond of money, as they say — poetical fact! I heard little else, except that the reign of Cant in England is growing wider and stronger each day. *John Bull* (the newspaper) attacked the licenser of the theatres for allowing a piece to pass with improper expressions, so the next farce was sent back to the theatre with a note from the Licenser to say that in the farce there were nine damns and two equivocal words which, considering

what *John Bull* said, he could not permit
to pass. *John Bull* is conducted by Hooke,
a man I know nothing of, but whom H. S.
and Kenny joined in abusing as the publisher and speaker of greater blasphemies,
indecencies, etc., than any person in the
world. My utter surprise is, why they
have not pounced upon *Valperga*.

Well! — they all seemed in a fright at
the idea of my being under the same roof
as Mrs. G. They made me promise (readily
enough) not to stay more than a few days
— "a few days in the Strand, and a few
weeks only in England." Mrs. K. said,
"you will be miserable there." My father,
it seems, is in excellent health, and generally
in good spirits; but *she* — well — Pazienza!
Kenny did not give a favourable account
of William either — vedremo. The Kennys
are to pay me a visit tomorrow, when I
may hear more.

I was pleased to see H. S. looking happy
and amiable (synonimes, Hunt?). I do
not know what to make of her; the only
thing that pleased me was a certain activity
of spirit she seemed to have — one likes
motion and life. Do you know that S.
gets two hundred pounds per annum from

Colburn, clear, regularly, for writing "al suo aggio" — some times yes, at times no — for the New Monthly. Would not such be a comfortable addition? If it were not too great an addition to Head Work — they want amusing and light writing so much, that they are ready to pay anything for it. Speak the word and I will try to manage it for you. It would be better than writing notes for the Italian selection — or that might be done in a more lucrative way. Shall I offer Colburn, by the bye, that selection? Going to the fountain head of the knowledge, I found that it was not true that the ladies were frightened at the first appearance of *Frankenstein*. K. says that the first appearance of the monster from F's laboratory down a dark staircase had a fine effect; but the piece fell off afterwards, though it is having a run.

I have just made my bargain for Calais, and go Wednesday noon (this is Monday). I shall arrive next Sunday, and hope to sail the day after. I am under a little anxiety about my finances, but trust that I have *just* enough to conclude my journey. I am obliged to travel rather more ex-pensively than I otherwise should, because my health will not permit me to travel at night. I am so very weak that the slightest exertion almost upsets me, and an emotion throws me into a fever. There was m——[music] at Kenny's and all at once I heard chords on the harp — the accompaniment of the Indian air you have so often heard me mention that [Shelley and] Jane used to sing together. One is so afraid of appearing affected, but I was obliged to entreat them to cease, and then smothered my tears and pain, for it darted like a spasm through me in my corner. It was the *only* air except one other of E's in the world, I think, that I could not have heard through without exposing myself; but how could I hear the *mimickry* of that voice! The witch, to recall such scenes! Let me forget it — the very remembrance makes me melancholy. Well then, *quatrini;* I trust that I have sufficient — and enough is as good as a *feast*, they say — so I shall be economical, without being anxious, for there is no use in that. I will write my last *un*-English letter to you from Calais.

My dearest Hunt, your letters are a great consolation to me. I feel remorse at the idea of you making your temples

beat and your head ache to please me;
but how can I forgo your kindness? And
when I get to England what else but those
and the hope of returning to Italy, can
keep up my spirits? And when I see
Italy receding and hope fail, what but
your letters, my best friend, have I left in
the world? You are the tie of the past,
the assurance of the future — my pardoner
and teacher. Well, I will not be too senti-
mental, though affection may excuse my
feeling, and bodily weakness and solitude
the expression. Goodnight. I will finish
my letter tomorrow.

(August 19th). — The Kennys have been
with me again today and I cannot refrain
from telling you what they told me of
Hazlitt. Just before the S. divorce he
met Mrs. H. in the street — "Ah, you
here — and how do you do?" "Oh, very
well, William, and how are you?" "Very
well, thank you. I was just looking about
for my dinner." "Well, mine is just ready
— a nice boiled leg of pork — if you like,
William, to have a slice." So he went and
had a slice. Miss Lamb in vain endeavoured to make her look on her journey to
Scotland in any other light than a jaunt.

K. met H. in the Hamstead fields — "Well
sir," he said — "I was just going to Mr. ——
there's a young lady there I don't know." —
"But," said K. "there was another, a
young lady of colour you were about to
marry — has she jilted you like Infelice?"
— "No, sir, but you see sir, she had relations — kind of people who ask after character, and as mine's small, sir, why it was
broken off." — K. says that when he met
you it was at Lamb's after a damnation
of his case — when all his wish was that
people *would not be sympathizing,* and that
you seemed to understand this feeling so
well and ate your supper with much appetite, and forced the conversation into the
most opposite channels that he was quite
delighted. "Yes," said Mrs. K., "I loved
Mr. Hunt from that moment." They
both desire to know more of you, and as
they talk of Italy next year, who knows?
K. is passionately fond of music — Mozart,
and Louisa plays uncommonly well. I am
more pleased with her the more I see her.
She and K. will probably come to Paris
tomorrow to take leave of me and perhaps
accompany me a few miles out of town.
I worked myself into good spirits this

afternoon and it would have been pleasant but for two young ladies whom Mrs. K. has under her care — They are romantic (ugly, mind you) and talk about happiness — ridicule the narrow prejudices of K. and L. who say that it consists in cheerfully fulfilling your duties and making those happy around you. "No," they say, "there will be no happiness in the world till every thing is capable of demonstration." Do you understand this? They seek their demonstration in balls, theatres, finery and their notions of romance, and treating ill a poor indulgent father, who is looked upon as the most prejudiced of beings. Miss Lamb, it seems, has attacks of a much lighter nature than formerly. She is never violent, and is never removed from home. She has a person to attend her there — she was ill for three months when in France in Mrs. K's house.

One more letter from Calais and then "to England if you will." Dear children, when shall your exile-Grandmother see you again! *They say that my father is anxious to see me — I dread that tie* — all the rest is air! Adieu, dearest Pollie; my good chicks I hope you are all good

121

T.J.M.L.P.H.S. and V. a blessing on you all. My dear Hunt, adieu; believe me
Faithfully yours,
MARY W. SHELLEY

Mrs. K. says that I am grown very like my mother, especially in manners — in my way of addressing people. This is the most flattering thing any one could say of me. I have tried to please them and I have some hope that I have succeeded.

H. S. tells me that L. T. S. is laid on the shelf and Whitton [1] and Lady S[helley]

---

[1] Sir Timothy Shelley's solicitor.

The following extract from a letter of Sir Timothy Shelley, of February 6, 1823, is of interest here. Lord Byron, as Shelley's executor, had made application to him for an allowance for his son's widow and child. — "I must decline all interference with matters in which Mrs. Shelley is interested. As to the child, I am inclined to afford the means of a suitable protection and care of him in this country if he shall be placed with a person I shall approve." On receipt of this information from Lord Byron Mrs. Shelley wrote — "He does not offer him an asylum in his own house, but a beggarly provision under the care of a stranger! Setting aside that, I would not part with him. Something is due me. I should not live ten days separated from him. . . . ; nor shall he be deprived of my anxious love and assiduous attention to his happiness while I have it in my power to bestow it on him; not to mention that his future respect for his father and his moral well-being greatly depend upon his being away from the immediate influence of his relations." Three years later she recorded the death of Shelley's eldest son Charles, by his first wife, which left her son Percy heir

122

manage every thing.   L. B. wanted me to
write to her.   I did not, for one hates to
beg.   Should I or not?   Tell me you, good
one.

9th September 1823 [1]

My dear Hunt: —

Bessy promised me to relieve you from
any inquietude you might suffer from not
hearing from me, so I indulged myself with
not writing to you until I was quietly
settled in lodgings of my own.   Want of
time is not my excuse: I had plenty, but,
until I saw all quiet around me, I had not
the spirit to write a line.   I thought of
you all — how much? and often longed to
write, yet would not till I called myself
free to turn southward; to imagine you
all, to put myself in the midst of you,
would have destroyed all my philosophy.
But now I do so.   I am in little neat
lodgings, my boy in bed, I quiet, and I
will now talk to you, tell you what I have
seen and heard, and with as little repining

to the baronetcy. Later, Sir Timothy's heart apparently
softened and he granted Mrs. Shelley a conditional allowance
of one hundred pounds, which was afterwards doubled; and
when Percy attained his majority and took his degree he
received an unconditional allowance of four hundred pounds.

[1] Mary had returned to England the last of August.

as I can, try (by making the best of what I have, the certainty of your friendship and kindness) to rest half content that I am not in the "Paradise of Exiles." Well, first I will tell you, journalwise, the history of my sixteen days in London.

I arrived Monday, the 25th of August. My Father and William came for me to the wharf. I had an excellent passage of eleven hours and a half, a glassy sea, and a contrary wind. The smoke of our fire was wafted right aft, and streamed out behind us; but wind was of little consequence; the tide was with us, and though the engine gave a "short uneasy motion" to the vessel, the water was so smooth that no one on board was sick, and Persino played about the deck in high glee. I had a very kind reception in the Strand, and all was done that could be done to make me comfortable. I exerted myself to keep up my spirits. The house, though rather dismal, is infinitely better than the Skinner Street one. I resolved not to think of certain things, to take all as a matter of course, and thus contrive to keep myself out of the gulf of melancholy, on the edge of which I was and am continually peeping.

But lo and behold! I found myself famous. *Frankenstein* had prodigious success as a drama, and was about to be repeated, for the twenty-third night, at the English Opera House. The play-bill amused me extremely, for, in the list of *dramatis personae*, came "——, by Mr. T. Cooke." This nameless mode of naming the unnameable is rather good.

On Friday, 29th August, Jane, my Father, William, and I went to the theatre to see it. Wallack looked very well as Frankenstein. He is at the beginning full of hope and expectation. At the end of the first act the stage represents a room with a staircase leading to Frankenstein's workshop; he goes to it, and you see his light at a small window, through which a frightened servant peeps, who runs off in terror when Frankenstein exclaims "It lives!" Presently Frankenstein himself rushes in horror and trepidation from the room, and, while still expressing his agony and terror, "——" throws down the door of the laboratory, leaps the staircase, and presents his unearthly and monstrous person on the stage. The story is not well managed, but Cooke played ——'s part extremely well; his seeking, as it were, for support; his trying to grasp at the sounds he heard; all, indeed, he does was well imagined and executed. I was much amused, and it appeared to excite a breathless eagerness in the audience. It was a third piece, a scanty pit filled at half-price, and all stayed till it was over. They continue to play it even now.

On Saturday, 30th August, I went with Jane to the Gisbornes. I know not why, but seeing them seemed more than anything else to remind me of Italy. Evening came on drearily, the rain splashed on the pavement, nor star nor moon deigned to appear. I looked upward to seek an image of Italy, but a blotted sky told me only of my change. I tried to collect my thoughts, and then, again, dared not think, for I am a ruin where owls and bats live only, and I lost my last *singing bird* when I left Albaro. It was my birthday, and it pleased me to tell the people so; to recollect and feel that time flies, and what is to arrive is nearer, and my home not so far off as it was a year ago. This same evening, on my return to the Strand, I saw Lamb, who was very entertaining and amiable, though a little deaf. One of the first questions he asked me was, whether they made puns in Italy: I said, "Yes, now Hunt is there." He said that Burney made a pun in Otaheite, the first that was ever made in that country. At first the natives could not make out what he meant, but all at once they discovered the *pun*, and danced round him in transports of joy. . . .

. . . On the strength of the drama, my Father had published for my benefit a new edition of *Frankenstein*, for he despaired utterly of my doing anything with Sir Timothy Shelley. I wrote to him, however, to tell him of my arrival, and on the following Wednesday had a note from Whitton, where he invited me, if I wished for an explanation of Sir T. Shelley's intentions concerning my boy, to call on him. I went with my Father. Whitton was very polite, though long-winded: his great wish seemed to be to prevent my applying again to Sir T. Shelley, whom he represented as old, infirm, and irritable. However, he advanced me one hundred pounds for my immediate expenses, told me that he could not speak positively until he had seen Sir T. Shelley, but that he doubted not but that I should receive the same annually for my child, and, with a little time and patience, I should get an allowance for myself. This, you see, relieved me from a load of anxieties.

Having secured neat cheap lodgings, we removed hither last night. Such, dear Hunt, is the outline of your poor exile's history. After two days of rain, the weather has been *uncommonly* fine, *cioè*, without rain, and cloudless, I believe, though I trusted to other eyes for that fact, since the white-washed sky is anything but blue to any but the perceptions of the natives themselves. It is so cold, however, that the fire I am now sitting by is not the first that has been lighted, for my father had one two days ago. The wind is east and piercing, but I comfort myself with the hope that softer gales are now fanning your *not* throbbing temples; that the climate of Florence will prove kindly to you, and that your health and spirits will return to you. Why am I not there? This is quite a foreign country to me, the names of the places sound strangely, the voices of the people are

new and grating, the vulgar English they
speak particularly displeasing. But for my
Father, I should be with you next spring,
but his heart and soul are set on my stay,
and in this world it always seems one's
duty to sacrifice one's own desires, and
that claim ever appears the strongest
which claims such a sacrifice.

London, 27th November, 1823

My dearest Polly: —

Are you not a naughty girl? How could
you copy a letter to that "agreeable,
unaffected woman, Mrs. Shelley," without
saying a word from yourself to your loving . . . . ? My dear Polly, a line from
you forms a better picture for me of what
you are about than — alas! I was going
to say three pages, but I check myself —
the rare one page of Hunt. Do you think
that I forget you — even Percy does not,
and he often tells me to bid the Signor
Enrico and you to get in a carriage and
then into a boat, and to come to *questo
paese* with *Baby nuovo*, Henry, Swinburne,
e tutti. But that will not be, nor shall I
see you at Mariano; this is a dreary exile
for me. During a long month of cloud

and fog, how often have I sighed for my beloved Italy, and more than ever this day when I have come to a conclusion with Sir Timothy Shelley as to my affairs, and I find the miserable pittance I am to have. Nearly sufficient in Italy, here it will not go half-way. It *is* one hundred pounds per annum. Nor is this all, for I foresee a thousand troubles; yet, in truth, as far as regards mere money matters and worldly prospects, I keep up my philosophy with excellent success. Others wonder at this, but I do not, nor is there any philosophy in it. After having witnessed the mortal agonies of my two darling children, after that journey from and to Lerici, I feel all these as pictures and trifles as long as I am kept out of contact with the unholy. I was upset to-day by being obliged to see Whitton, and the prospect of seeing others of his tribe. I can earn a sufficiency, I doubt not. In Italy I should be content: here I will not bemoan. Indeed I never do, and Mrs. Godwin makes *large eyes* at the quiet way in which I take it all. It is England alone that annoys me, yet sometimes I get among friends and almost forget its fogs. I go to Shacklewell rarely, and sometimes see the Novellos elsewhere. He is my especial favourite, and his music always transports me to the seventh heaven. . . . I see the Lambs rather often, she ever amiable, and Lamb witty and delightful. I must tell you one thing and make Hunt laugh. Lamb's new house at Islington is close to the New River, and George Dyer, after having paid them a visit, on going away at 12 noonday, walked deliberately into the water, taking it for the high road. "But," as he said afterwards to Proctor, "I soon found that I was in the water, sir." So Miss Lamb and the servant had to fish him out. . . . I must tell Hunt also a good saying of Lamb's, —talking of some one, he said, "Now some men who are very veracious are called matter-of-fact men, but such a one I should call a matter-of-lie man."

I have seen also Procter, with his "beauti- fully formed head" (it is beautifully formed), several times, and I like him. He is an enthusiastic admirer of Shelley, and most zealous in bringing out the volume of his poems; this alone would please me; and he is, moreover, gentle and gentle- manly, and apparently endued with a true poetic feeling. Besides, he is an invalid, and some time ago I told you, in a letter, that I have always a sneaking (for sneaking read open) kindness for men of literary and particularly poetic habits, who have delicate health. I cannot help revering the mind delicately attuned that shatters the material frame, and whose thoughts are strong enough to throw down and dilapidate the walls of sense and dikes of flesh that the unimaginative contrive to keep in such good repair. . . .

After all, I spend a great deal of my time in solitude. I have been hitherto too fully occupied in preparing Shelley's MSS. It is now complete, and the poetry alone will make a large volume. Will you tell Hunt that he need not send any of the MSS. that he has (except the Essay on Devils, and some lines addressed to himself on his arrival in Italy, if he should choose them to be inserted), as I have recopied all the rest? We should be very glad, however, of his notice as quickly as possible, as we wish the book to be out in a month at furthest, and that will not be possible unless he sends it immediately. It would break my heart if the book should

appear without it.[1] When he does send a
packet over (let it be directed to his
brother), will he also be so good as to send
me a copy of my "Choice," beginning
after the line

Entrenched sad lines, or blotted with its might?

Perhaps, dear Marianne, you would have
the kindness to copy them for me, and
send them soon. I have another favour
to ask of you. Miss Curran has a portrait
of Shelley, in many things very like, and
she has so much talent that I entertain
great hopes that she will be able to make a
good one; for this purpose I wish her to
have all the aids possible, and among the
rest a profile from you.[2] If you could not
cut another, perhaps you would send her
one already cut, and if you sent it with a
note requesting her to return it when she
had done with it, I will engage that it will
be most faithfully returned. At present
I am not quite sure where she is, but if
she should be there, and you can find her

[1] So it happened, however.
[2] Mrs. Hunt, an amateur sculptress of talent, was also
skillful in cutting out profiles in cardboard. From some of
these, notably from one of Lord Byron, successful likenesses
were made.

133

and send her this, I need not tell you how you would oblige me.

I heard from Bessy that Hunt is writing something for the *Examiner* for me. I *conjecture* that this may be concerning *Valperga.* I shall be glad, indeed, when that comes, or in lieu of it, anything else. John Hunt begins to despair. . . .

And now, dear Polly, I think I have done with gossip and business: with words of affection and kindness I should never have done. I am inexpressibly anxious about you all. Percy has had a similar though shorter attack to that at Albaro, but he is now recovered. I have a cold in my head, occasioned, I suppose, by the weather. Ah, Polly! if all the beauties of England were to have only the mirror that Richard III desires, a very short time would be spent at the looking-glass!

What of Florence and the gallery? I saw the Elgin marbles today; to-morrow I am to go to the Museum to look over the prints: that will be a great treat. The Theseus is a divinity, but how very few statues they have! Kiss the children. Ask Thornton for his forgotten and promised P. S., give my love to Hunt, and

believe me, my dear Marianne, the exiled,
but ever, most affectionately yours,

MARY W. SHELLEY

Feb. 9th, London [1824]

My dear Hunt —

I intend to write you but a short letter,
and should even have deferred writing at
all but that we have begun to print and I
am anxious to receive your MS. As in
the latter part of your letter you say that
you will send it immediately upon my
asking for it I need hardly answer what
you say about putting off the publication
for a year. Alas, my dear friend, "there
is a tide in the affairs of men"; Shelley
has celebrity, even popularity, now. A
winter ago greater interest would perhaps
have been excited than now by this volume,
but who knows what may happen before
the next? Indeed I have given my word
to several people; it has been advertised,
and moreover, do you, my best friend,
assist me in making it complete. Send
me what you prepare, for it is not yet too
late; but if you wait to exchange more
letters it will be.

I am very glad to hear that my good

Polly has written and that I am to have
the letter — si dio vuole — some time or
other; and I wish that in return I could
send you a budget of good news. But
what is there good in the world, and above
all [this] miserable country. The Novellos
are at Shacklewell; they have just [moved
what] remained of their furniture from
Percy Street, and Mrs. N. has been so
engaged in arranging that I have not seen
much of them for nearly a month. I saw
the Lambs last night and they were quite
well. Mrs. Williams is well, but as im-
patient as I of England and the rest of it.
She bears herself up very well, but it is
very, very hard to fall from the enjoyment
of life to a living death. You have of
course heard of the event of your brother's
trial. All the world cries out about it,
and the Court itself seems displeased with
the officiousness of the prosecutors; yet
twelve men were found who could give a
verdict of guilty. The judgment is not
yet passed, and probably will not be yet
awhile, for the judges say that they have
too much to do — casting an eye perhaps
on a paper which your brother holds when
he attends their Lordship's leisure, and not

knowing how long they may be kept. Do not frown at this *scherzo* — upon the whole I am much prepossessed in your brother's favour. He called on me the day before he expected to be sent to prison — expressed his great pleasure in your having agreed to his arrangements, and evinced a sensibility in his manner of which I did not judge him capable. Poor fellow! he is hardly used in this world; but così va il mondo.

Do you know I have drawn on him for his theatrical ticket for D[rury] L[ane] till I am half ashamed, and yet go on. The truth is, I have been highly delighted with Kean; he excites me and makes me happy for the time, and in addition the idea of writing a tragedy, "*that last infirmity of noble minds,*" has come over me — and though as yet I have thrown all my halting verses in to the fire, yet I still dream of the buskined muse and see Kean partly as a study. I wish to do anything to get rid of my enemies — the blue devils! — I try hard; every now and then I cut off a head of the hydra, but two pop up instead of one *ed ecconii li.*

I spoke to your brother about the

Bacchus — he said that he had offered it to Colburn, who declined, and meant to offer it to others. I will see him soon about it and try what can be done. Ultra Crepidarius does not sell; Gifford is out of fashion — quite forgotten — and even your lines will not stir the waters of oblivion in which he has sunk. Write your articles, with your *Indicators* — your wishing cap — it is thus you will make money, the grand desideratum with us grovelling mortals. As for me, bien mauvais grè, I write bad articles which help to make me miserable, but I am going to plunge into a novel, and hope that its clear waters will wash off the mud of the magazine.

Oh that you would answer a letter! Perhaps Marianne will. What of Miss Curran? [1] What of the promised profile of my Shelley? What of his verses to you? You ask me what authority I have for asking for Trelawny's letters. I only

[1] Miss Curran was the artist who painted Shelley's portrait in Rome — the only authentic portrait of him in existence. After much vexatious delay and letter-writing, Mrs. Shelley received the portrait, and on September 17, 1825, she records it in her journal — "Thy picture is come, my only one. Thine, those speaking eyes, that animated look; unlike aught earthly wert thou ever, and art now!"

asked for one, and it was because he referred me to it in one to me and said that he hoped you would send it.

This is a shabby letter. I write at this moment only to entreat you to send the notice for our volume (send it directed to your brother) as soon as possible. Adieu, good friends. Be well happy and good; so prays your exiled grandmother.

MARY SHELLEY

(Direct to me at John Hunt's as I am about to change my lodgings).

London, June 13th [1824]

My best Polly —

You perhaps will wonder that you have not heard from me; while I have been lost in conjecture as to occasion of Hunt's silence. All I can say in my excuse is this: I have now a letter open before me addressed to you, dated May 9th, beginning with these words: "I have delayed writing in expectation of an answer from Hunt; the delay on his part gives me hopes that he will treat me at last with kindness and confidence and send me his MS. In the mean time I will fill two sides of my paper and then leave the third blank for some days more, in hopes that I may then fill it with acknowledgments for his envoy." This luckless third page was filled up on June 1st. I then sealed my letter, and annoying circumstances have prevented my sending it, till now I begin to think that I had better write another, at which task behold me occupied.

It is fifty ages since I heard any news of you, and I long excessively for a letter — how much more do I long that I were with you! Truly my mode of life in England is little agreeable to me; my only comfort is in my child's growth and health and in the society of Mrs. Williams. She has been seriously indisposed the whole winter and it is only on her recent removal from the smoke of London to Kentish Town (12 Mortimer Terrace!) that she has begun to recover. She is so thin, and then she in no way gives herself up, but struggles against debility and ill health to the very last, and is as cheerful as she can be in this cloudy land. The Natives call it summer, while they, as well as I, shiver . . . — the fields may well be green, being well watered, and when it does rain, Nature kindly preserves their complexion by suspending over them a sunproof parasol of clouds. Yet, dear Hunt (if so, not being angry with me, you allow me to call you), the fields on the two!!! fine days we have had were superbly beautiful. I walked to Hamstead Heath on one of them, and on another through the meadows which divide Hamstead from the Regent's Park, and so home by Kentish Town. The smell of hay perfumed the air, the soft tall green grass starred by "buttercups that will be seen, whether you will see or no," the elms and grassy lanes all brought old times to my mind. I long to get out to K. T. when I shall be near my Janey, but circumstances obliged me to delay my removal until the beginning of June, and now I cannot get lodgings there. In the mean time I enjoy (when it does not rain) all I can of the country, by help of prodigious walks. Ye Gods, how I walk! and starve — because in spite of all I am too much *embon point* — Cosa vuole? quel che dio vuole, sara, e ci vuol pazienza. My walks some times turn towards Shacklewell, that dreary flat, scented by brick kilns and adorned by carcasses of houses. The good kind hearts that inhabit it com-

141

pensate for it, when once arrived, but it prevents frequent visits, and Mrs. Novello's *circumstance* (as Pamela calls it) now almost entirely prevents her from coming to town. You will not see them in Italy this summer. I can bear witness that is not Mrs. N's, but Vincenzo's fault — he says that if he could bring you all back with him he would not hesitate; but his time would be so short, the way so long, and his pain at leaving you so great, that he puts the ounce of sweet meeting in an opposite scale to the pound of bitter parting, and lo! the smiles kick the beam and the sighs enchain him here. The Gliddons are evidently a good deal cut up by the removal of their friends; they go there in the rain and return home weary, and the N's say that they will come — and then they do not. In fact the great pleasure of friendship, constant intercourse, is inevitably destroyed. Statia (the "yes, Mrs. Hunt") is grown into a fine tall girl, and though she may not be brilliant, is far from silly.

I cannot conjecture, I own, why Hunt refused to join his name to mine in my publication. I have been too little accustomed to be treated with suspicion, and am far too secure that I do not deserve it, to know how to conduct myself when treated thus unjustly; that is to say, if suspicion has been the cause of his refusal. I hope that you will soon receive a copy; and I hope that the preface will at least not displease him; and yet it may, although I have done my best that it should not. During the dreary winter I passed at Genoa, in the midst of coldness and aversion I preserved my affection for Hunt. Suspicion is deadly poison to friendship, but I will give mine *patience* as an antidote, and my naughty boy (patient no longer) is and must [ever] be dear to me — even though he disclaims me, as he does.

Have you heard from Trelawny? I am very anxious to have a letter, since none has been received by him since that which you forwarded. I wish that he had been at Missalunghi, since I doubt not that want of proper attendance caused the melancholy catastrophe of L. B.'s voyage, and his activity and kindness might have prevented it. We have heard from Clare since I wrote — poor girl! She is dismally tossed about,[1]

[1] It will be remembered that Clare accompanied Mary when she eloped with Shelley. He never forgot that favor,

so much so that perhaps she may return to England. To exchange Italy for England is dreary work, but it must be pleasanter than Moscow after all. I think this is all the news that I can tell you. It is very, very long since I have seen Procter; he is much annoyed by his affairs and also by ill health. C. Lamb has suspended his Elias. My father's first volume of the History of the Commonwealth has come out and sells well, I believe. I hope by next spring to publish myself, and shall work hard the moment I get into country lodgings; and before, if my removal continues to be delayed.

And what do you all do with yourselves? Out of Florence, you must lead very recluse lives, and I fear all your spirits suffer from want of society. I see few, but those few often. Now Kean plays no more, my only public amusement is the Opera, which is inexpressibly delightful to me. Good people of England have shown taste in it. Notwithstanding Rossini being the fashion and his going to

of her giving up her own mother to accompany them, and in his will he bequeathed her twelve thousand pounds from the estates that he should afterwards inherit. It was paid to her on the death of Sir Timothy.

Carlton House and giving concerts under
the patronage of the ladies of Almacks,
the singers have each chosen Mozart for
their Benefit. That nice creature la Cara-
dori began it by selecting Don Giovanni
for hers, and played Zerlina as well (and
that is saying every thing) as la Fodor.
Garcia was the Don — in one or two parts
he surpassed Ambrogetti, but in others
(in la ci darem particularly) he put me in
mind of the *Union of Voices,* he was so full
of graces — and then he pronounces Italian
vilely: il Begnis made an enchanting
Leperello; he is full of comic talent, and
truly Italian. La Catalani took Le Nozzi
di Figaro for her benefit. We had an
odious page, but the rest was good. The
pretty la Begnis made a sweet countess —
and Begnis's singing of *Le vuol calare* was
incomparable. *Sul'aria* was encored, of
course; there are one or two excellent airs
in this piece which are spoiled because
they devolve on inferior singers — La Ven-
detta, for instance, which Francesco Novello
fills full [of] animation and beauty is lost
in the stupid Bartolo of the Opera. The
town is extremely full — there are exhibi-
tions of all kinds — two of the ruined city

145

of Pompeii — which the painter has spoiled by covering the glowing earth with an English sky. There are several fine old paintings which are to me drops of water in the desert. The Llandes bring all Italy before my eyes and thus transport me to Paradise.

(June 15th). — After writing the above I went to St. P. Ch. Yd. to see Bessy concerning this début of your brother, and it is settled that I go with them on Thursday; so I shall not close this letter until this is decided. Your mother was infinitely nervous; she spoke with great delight of a letter that she had received from you. Bessy is so changed that you would hardly know her again; she is grown plump and contented-looking. This is the more wonderful as she continues to take opium, and could not leave it off without extreme suffering; but it seems to have no other effect on her than to keep her in good health. Nancy was remarkably blooming — her costume is somewhat altered and civilised — I have once or twice seen the nankeens — but white frocks, sashes, and pretty silk kerchiefs are permitted as well as curls — great innovations these. I heard yesterday from John Hunt that my volume promises to sell well. — If I do get, and when I get, money from it I will send you the things you desire; but I have only one hundred pounds p. a. from S. T. S. — enough in Italy, but only half enough for England. I shall see Virtue (i.e. Laura — are these synonymous since Petrarch's time?) on Thursday. Mrs. Williams is to go also, who is an extreme favourite of your mother. Adieu for the present.

(June 18th). — I own when I had finished so far, I began to tremble as to what this little space might contain; nor was I altogether comfortable at the idea of going with your mother and sister to witness Tom's defeat; but on the contrary, my dear, we beheld his most unequivocal triumph. The play was Richard III. I do not pretend to say that I like him as I do Kean, but of course he could not act his best on the first night. The first good point of his was. "Was ever woman in such humour won?" and the best thing he said during the whole night was, "Richard is himself again." After he died, not a word was to be heard, nor could Richmond in any way contrive to give out the play

147

for the next night; in fact one could not hear oneself speak, the hubbub was so tremendous. C. Kemble at length made Tom go on to meet their repeated calls for him. There was some opposition, but it came principally from the gallery. Poor Tom, as you may guess, is infinitely delighted to find himself, as he says, transformed from a poor to a rich man at once. He had refused an offer of eighteen pounds per week, and Kemble is now quite cap in hand to him.

When I see him again I shall judge better of his real merits — which one cannot do when he himself was agitated — and one's attention was of course as much directed towards the audience as towards him. Besides, we were (in a private box) a great way from the stage. His voice is the best on the stage, and that is the greatest thing in his favour. However, his acting (as I said) cannot be judged of by last night. Your mother behaved very well; she took your grandmother with us. The old lady sat as quiet and pleased as possible — Nancy was all anxiety, and Virtue sat pale and silent as Marble — or her namesake. Your mother told me to tell you that she would write as soon as she had found her wits. He is to play R. III. again on Monday. I had intended not to go, but if they of H. P.'s insist upon it, I will — though I had rather see him next in a new character.

Write soon, my Polly, if Hunt is inexorable and will not write again give my love to him, to Occhi Turchini and the rest.

Yours affectionately,

Mary W. S.

Kentish Town, 22d August, 1824

. . . A negotiation has begun between Sir Timothy Shelley and myself, by which, on sacrificing a small part of my future expectations on the will, I shall ensure myself a sufficiency for the present, and not only that, but be able, I hope, to relieve Clare from her disagreeable situation at Moscow. I have been obliged, however, as an indispensable preliminary, to suppress the posthumous poems. More than 300 copies had been sold, so this is the less provoking, and I have been obliged to promise not to bring dear Shelley's name before the public again during Sir Timothy's life. There is no great harm in this, since

149

he is above seventy; and, from choice, I should not think of writing memoirs now, and the materials for a volume of more works are so scant that I doubted before whether I could publish it. Such is the folly of the world, and so do things seem different from what they are; since, from Whitton's account, Sir Timothy writhes under the fame of his incomparable son, as if it were the most grievous injury done to him; and so, perhaps, after all it will prove.

All this was pending when I wrote last, but until I was certain I did not think it worth while to mention it. The affair is arranged by Peacock, who, though I seldom see him, seems anxious to do me all these kind of services in the best manner that he can.

It is long since I saw your brother, nor had he any news for me. I lead a most quiet life, and see hardly any one. The Gliddons are gone to Hastings for a few weeks. Hogg is on Circuit. Now that he is rich he is so very queer, so unamiable, and so strange, that I look forward to his return without any desire of shortening the term of absence.

Poor Pierino is now in London, *Non fosse male questo paese*, he says, *se vi vedesse mai il sole.* He is full of Greece, to which he is going, and gave us an account of our good friend, Trelawny, which was that he was not at all changed. Trelawny has made a hero of the Greek chief, Ulysses, and declares that there is a great cavern in Attica which he and Ulysses have provisioned for seven years, and to which, if the cause fails, he and this chieftain are to retire; but if the cause is triumphant, he is to build a city in the Negropont, colonise it, and Jane and I are to go out to be queens and chieftainesses of the island. When he first came to Athens he took to a Turkish life, bought twelve or fifteen women, *brutti mostri*, Pierino says, one a Moor, of all things! and there he lay on his sofa, smoking, these gentle creatures about him, till he got heartily sick of idleness, shut them up in his harem, and joined and combated with Ulysses. . . .

One of my principal reasons for writing just now is that I have just heard Miss Curran's address (64 Via Sistina, Roma), and I am anxious that Marianne should (if she will be so very good) send one of

the profiles already cut to her, of Shelley,
since I think that, by the help of that,
Miss Curran will be able to correct her
portrait of Shelley, and make for us what
we so much desire — a good likeness. I
am convinced that Miss Curran will return
the profile immediately that she has done
with it, so that you will not sacrifice it,
though you may be the means of our
obtaining a good likeness.

Kentish Town, 10th October, 1824
. . . I write to you on the most dismal
of all days, a rainy Sunday, when dreary
church-going faces look still more drearily
from under dripping umbrellas, and the
poor plebeian dame looks reproachfully at
her splashed white stockings, — not her
gown, — that has been warily held high up,
and the to-be-concealed petticoat has borne
all the ill-usage of the mud. Dismal though
it is, dismal though I am, I do not wish to
write a discontented letter, but in a few
words to describe things as they are with
me. A weekly visit to the Strand, a
monthly visit to Shacklewell (when we
are sure to be caught in the rain) forms my
catalogue of visits. I have no visitors;

if it were not for Jane I should be quite alone. The eternal rain imprisons one in one's little room, and one's spirits flag without one exhilarating circumstance. In some things, however, I am better off than last year, for I do not doubt but that in the course of a few months I shall have an independence; and I no longer balance, as I did last winter, between Italy and England. My father wished me to stay, and, old as he is, and wishing as one does to be of some use somewhere, I thought that I would make the trial, and stay if I could. But the joke has become too serious. I look forward to the coming winter with horror but it *shall* be the last. I have not yet made up my mind to the where in Italy. I shall, if possible, immediately on arriving, push on to Rome. Then we shall see. I read, study, and write; sometimes that takes me out of myself; but to live for no one, to be necessary to none, to know that "Where is now my hope? for my hope, who shall see it? They shall go down to the base of the pit, when our rest together is in the dust." But change of scene and the sun of Italy will restore my energy; the very thought

of it smooths my brow. Perhaps I shall
seek the heats of Naples, if they do not
hurt my darling Percy. And now, what
news? . . .

Hazlitt is abroad; he will be in Italy in
the winter; he wrote an article in the
Edinburgh Review on the volume of poems
I published. I do not know whether he
meant it to be favourable or not; I do not
like it at all; but when I saw him I could
not be angry. I never was so shocked in
my life; he has become so thin, his hair
scattered, his cheek-bones projecting; but
for his voice and smile I should not have
known him; his smile brought tears into
my eyes, it was like a sunbeam illuminating
the most melancholy of ruins, lightning
that assured you in a dark night of the
identity of a friend's ruined and deserted
abode. . . .

Have you, my Polly, sent a profile to
Miss Curran in Rome? Now pray do,
and pray write; do, my dear girl. Next
year by this time I shall, perhaps, be on
my way to you; it will go hard but that I
contrive to spend a week (that is, if you
wish) at Florence, on my way to the
Eternal City. God send that this prove

not an airy castle; but I own that I put faith in my having money before that; and I know that I could not, if I would, endure the torture of my English life longer than is absolutely necessary. By the bye, I heard that you are keeping your promise to Trelawny, and that in due time he will be blessed with a name-sake. How is *Occhi Turchini*, Thornton the reformed, Johnny the — what Johnny? the good boy? Mary the merry, Irving the sober, Percy the martyr, and dear Sylvan the good?

Percy is quite well; tell his friend he goes to school and learns to read and write, being very handy with his hands, perhaps having a pure anticipated cognition of the art of painting in his tiny fingers. Mrs. Williams's little girl, who calls herself Dina, is his wife. Poor Clare, at Moscow! at least she will be independent one day, and if I am so soon, her situation will be quickly ameliorated.

Have you heard of Medwin's book? Notes of conversations which he had with Lord Byron (when tipsy); every one is to be in it; every one will be angry. He wanted me to have a hand in it, but I declined. Years ago, when a man died, the worms ate him; now a new set of worms feed on the carcase of the scandal he leaves behind him, and grow fat upon the world's love of tittle-tattle. I will not be numbered among them.[1] Have you received the volume of poems? Give my love to "Very," and so, dear, very patient, Adieu. —

Yours affectionately,

MARY SHELLEY

8th April, 1825

My dear Hunt —

I have just finished reading your article upon Shelley. It is with great diffidence that I write to thank you for it, because perceiving plainly that you think that I have forfeited all claim on your affection, you may deem my thanks an impertinent intrusion. But from my heart I thank you. You may imagine that it has moved

[1] Hunt, however, was differently constituted. He had an imaginary grievance against Byron, and scarcely waited for the great poet to get cold in his grave before beginning an article on which he hoped to "grow fat" in a pecuniary way, at the expense of Byron's reputation. But the disingenuous article lost all its desired effect, due to the personal animosity and pettishness that characterized it from beginning to end.

me deeply. Of course this very article shows how entirely you have cast me out from any corner of your affections.[1] And from various causes — none dishonourable to me — I cannot help wishing that I could have received your goodwill and kindness, which I prize, and have ever prized; but you have a feeling, I had almost said a prejudice, against me, which makes you construe foreign matter into detractation against me (I allude to the — to me — deeply afflicting idea you got upon some vague expression communicated to you by your brother), and insensible to any circumstances that might be pleaded for me. But I will not dwell on this. The sun shines, and I am striving so hard for a continuation of the gleams of pleasure that visit my intolerable state of regret for the loss of beloved companionship during cloudless days, that I will dash away the springing tears and make one

[1] The article referred to was perhaps the one that soon afterwards appeared in Hunt's publication entitled *Lord Byron and Some of his Contemporaries.* Had Mrs. Shelley known of the sort of shallow, acrimonious "tittle-tattle" about Byron that was to be printed in the volume with the article on Shelley she would doubtless have felt that she could well afford to be left out of that book.

or two necessary observations on your article.

I have often heard our Shelley relate the story of stabbing an upper boy with a fork, but never as you relate it. He always described it, in my hearing, as being an almost involuntary act, done on the spur of anguish, and that he made the stab as the boy was going out of the room. Shelley did not allow Harriet half his income. She received two hundred pounds a year. Mr. Westbrook had always made his daughter an allowance, even while she lived with Shelley, which of course was continued to her after their separation. I think if I were near you, I could readily persuade you to omit all allusion to Clare. After the death of Lord Byron, in the thick of memoirs, scandal, and turning up of old stories, she has never been alluded to, at least in any work I have seen. You mention (having been obliged to return your MS. to Bowring, I quote from memory) an article in *Blackwood*, but I hardly think that this is of date subsequent to our miserable loss. In fact, poor Clare has been buried in entire oblivion, and to bring her from this, even for the sake of defending her, would, I am sure, pain her greatly, and do her mischief.[1] Would you permit this part to be erased? I have, without waiting to ask your leave, requested Messrs. Bowring to leave out your mention that the remains of dearest Edward were brought to England. Jane still possesses this treasure, and has once or twice been asked by his mother-in-law about it, — once an urn was sent. Consequently she is very anxious that her secret should be kept, and has allowed it to be believed that the ashes were deposited with Shelley's at Rome. Such, my dear Hunt, are all the alterations I have to suggest, and I lose no time in communicating them to you. They are too trivial for me to apologise for the liberty, and I hope that you will agree with me in what I say about Clare — Allegra no more — she at present absent and forgotten. On Sir Timothy's death she will come in for a legacy which may enable her to enter into society, — perhaps to marry, if she wishes it, if the past be forgotten.

[1] It must have cost Hunt a bitter pang to comply with this reasonable request, since it was about the only thing discreditable to Byron that he appeared to know about, and it robbed his diatribe of two hundred and forty odd pages of the only sting that would have hurt Byron's memory.

I forget whether such things are recorded by "Galignani," or, if recorded, whether you would have noticed it. My father's complicated annoyances, brought to their height by the failure of a very promising speculation and the loss of an impossible-to-be-lost law-suit, have ended in a bankruptcy, the various acts of which drama are now in progress; that over, nothing will be left to him but his pen and me. He is so full of his *Commonwealth* that in the midst of every anxiety he writes every day now, and in a month or two will have completed the second volume, and I am employed in raising money necessary for my maintenance, and in which he must participate. This will drain me pretty dry for the present, but (as the old women say) if I live, I shall have more than enough for him and me, and recur, at least to some part of my ancient style of life, and feel of some value to others. Do not, however, mistake my phraseology; I shall not live with my Father, but return to Italy and economise, the moment God and Mr. Whitton will permit. My Percy is quite well, and has exchanged his constant winter occupation of drawing for playing in the

fields (which are now useful as well as orna-
mental), flying kites, gardening, etc. I bask
in the sun on the grass reading Virgil; that
is, my beloved Georgics and Lord Shaftes-
bury's *Characteristics.* I begin to live again,
and as the maids of Greece sang joyous
hymns on the revival of Adonais, does my
spirit lift itself in delightful thanksgiving
on the awakening of nature.

Lamb is superannuated — do you understand? as Madame says. He has left the
India House on two-thirds of his income,
and become a gentleman at large — a
delightful consummation. What a strange
taste it is that confines him to a view of
the New River, with houses opposite, in
Islington! I saw the Novellos the other
day. Mary and her new babe are well;
he, Vincent all over, fat and flourishing
moreover, and she dolorous that it should
be her fate to add more than her share to
the population of the world. How are all
yours — Henry and the rest? Percy still
remembers him, though occupied by new
friendships and the feelings incident to his
state of matrimony, having taken for
better and worse to wife Mrs. Williams's
little girl.

161

I suppose you will receive with these letters Bessy's new book, which she has done very well indeed, and forms with the other a delightful prize for plant and flower worshippers, those favourites of God, which enjoy beauty unequalled and the tranquil pleasures of growth and life, bestowing incalculable pleasure, and never giving or receiving pain. Have you seen Hazlitt's notes of his travels? He is going over the same road that I have travelled twice. He surprised me by calling the road from Susa to Turin dull; there, where the Alps sink into low mountains and romantic hills, topped by ruined castles, watered by brawling streams, clothed by magnificent walnut trees; there where I wrote to you in a fit of enchantment, exalted by the splendid scene; but I remembered, first, that he travelled in winter, when snow covers all; and, besides, he went from what I approached, and looked at the plain of Lombardy with the back of the diligence between him and the loveliest scene in nature; so much can *relation* alter circumstances.

Clare is still, I believe, at Moscow. When I return to Italy I shall endeavour

to enable her to go thither also. I shall
not come without my Jane, who is now
necessary to my existence almost. She
has recourse to the cultivation of her mind,
and amiable and dear as she ever was, she
is in every way improved and become more
valuable.

Trelawny is in the cave with Ulysses, not
in Polypheme's cave, but in a vast cavern
of Parnassus; inaccessible and healthy
and safe, but cut off from the rest of the
world. Trelawny has attached himself to
the part of Ulysses, a savage chieftain,
without any plan but personal independence and opposition to the Government. Trelawny calls him a hero. Ulysses
speaks a word or two of French; Trelawny, no Greek! Pierino has returned to
Greece.

Horace Smith has returned with his
diminished family (little Horace is dead).
He already finds London too expensive,
and they are about to migrate to Tun-
bridge Wells. He is very kind to me.

I long to hear from you, and I am more
tenderly attached to you and yours than
you imagine; love me a little, and make
Marianne love me, as truly I think she does.

163

Am I mistaken, Polly? — Yours affectionate and obliged,

MARY W. SHELLEY

Kentish Town, June 27 [1825]

My dear Hunt —

You can hardly be more delighted at the idea of returning to Tottenham Court Road and the Hampstead Coachmen, than are your friends that you should return, and return with pleasure, to these things. If you were here just now you would find England in all its glory, and the people complaining of the Italian heat of the weather; though like me, I think you would find *qualche differenza*. But the English expose themselves to the sunny sides of the way at noon and then are angry to find it too warm.

Of course all questions of the future are rife among us. Where will they live? — I told the N's that I thought that you would take Shacklewell on your shoulders and bear it Westward. *You* could not live there — you who come for the sake of green fields would not be content with drab-coloured meadows and brick kilns. I saw Novello on Sunday and had a long

talk with him about you. He desired me
to send the kindest messages; and his
renovated spirits and health show with
what eagerness he looks forward to the
enjoyment of your society. But he told
me to entreat you not to set out until
you should hear from him again; as he is
very anxious to arrange your debts before
your arrival. He is a true, ardent and
faithful friend to you. I think that your
arrival will do them a great deal of good,
for poor Mary by going to that place has
shut herself out from society and pines;
and Vincent has headaches in solitude.
You ask about their children; you know I
cannot tell of the advancement of your
knowledge on the subject, so for fear of
being puzzling I will "tell the tale" —
Victoria, now at Boulogne and not to
return; Alfred in Yorkshire; Cecilia, Edward about to go to Hazlewood; Emma,
Clara, Mary, and Florence — the little boy,
Charles Arthur, brought into the world last
autumn died a month ago in consequence of
a fall. He was a thriving child and this
misfortune cut them up a good deal, until
revived by the hopes of your return. Such
is a full true and particular account.

This does not intend to be a long letter or an answer to your last. When we meet, if the Gods permit, I will tell you one or two things which will, I think, surprize and perhaps move you — move you at least to excuse a little what you do not approve. I continue to live in quietness — the hope and consolation of my life is the society of Mrs. W[illiams]. To her, for better or worse, I am wedded — while she will have me, and I continue in the lovelorn state that I have since I returned to this native country of yours. I go or stay as she or rather our joint circumstances decide — which now with ponderous chain and heavy log enroot us in Kentish Town. I think of Italy as of a vision of delight afar off, and go to the Opera sometimes merely for the sake of seeing my dear Italians and listening to that glorious language in its perfection.

Where will you live, my dear Hunt, and my Polly? And what will you do? — Command me, I entreat you — if it be that I can be of the slightest use to you. I am pleased to think that Penino (who does not understand a word of Italian) will renew his friendship with your sweet Henry. I long to see Occhi Turchini, and

166

to congratulate Thornton, when he shall be fairly established in an arm chair with his Bingley. Where will you live? Near Hampstead — not in Hampstead perhaps; it is so dear, and so far — but on the road to it, I think you might be accommodated. There are some empty houses on Mortimer Terrace, but I believe my good Polly does not like that. My Polly, I traverse the gap fearless at ten at night and Jane and I in some of our disastrous journies to see our friends, have passed it much later. Mafaccian loro — We'll talk Tuscan, Hunt, and I shall get more sick than ever for valle che de miei lamenti son pieni. So you are about to bid adieu to fireflies, azioli, the Tuscan peasantry and Tuscan vines! But no more of that — our feelings are so different and we have each such excellent reasons for the difference of our feelings on this subject, that we may differ and agree — the same is not the same you know. Had you seen Italy as I saw it — had I seen it as you — we should each be delighted with our present residence, nor for the world's treasure change.

Adieu, dear Hunt, and love.

Yours faithfully,

MARY SHELLEY

167

5 Bartholomew Place, Kentish Town,
30th October, 1826

My dear Hunt —

Is it, or is it not, right that these few lines should be addressed to you now? Yet if the subject be one that you may judge better to have been deferred, set my *delay* down to the account of over-zeal in writing to relieve you from a part of the care which I know is just now oppressing you; too happy I shall be if you permit any act of mine to have that effect.

I told you long ago that our dear Shelley intended, on rewriting his will, to have left you a legacy. I think the sum mentioned was two thousand pounds. I trust that hereafter you will not refuse to consider me your debtor for this sum merely because I shall be bound to pay it you by the laws of honour instead of a legal obligation. You would, of course, have been better pleased to have received it immediately from dear Shelley's bequest; but as it is well known that he intended to make such an one, it is in fact the same thing, and so I hope by you to be considered; besides, your kind heart will receive pleasure from the knowledge that you are bestowing on me the greatest pleasure I am capable of receiving. This is no resolution of today, but formed from the moment I knew my situation to be such as it is. I did not mention it, because it seemed almost like an empty vaunt to talk and resolve on things so far off. But futurity approaches, and a feeling haunts me as if this futurity were not far distant.[1] I have spoken vaguely to you on this subject before, but now, you having had a recent disappointment, I have thought it as well to inform you in express terms of the meaning I attached to my expressions. I have as yet made no will, but in the meantime, if I should chance to die, this present writing may serve as a legal document to prove that I give and bequeath to you the sum of two thousand pounds sterling. But I hope we shall both live, I to acknowledge dear Shelley's intentions, you to honour me so far as to permit me to be their executor.

I have mentioned this subject to no one, and do not intend; an act is not aided by words, especially an act unfulfilled, nor

[1] Sir Timothy far outlived their expectations. He clung tenaciously to life until 1844.

does this letter, methinks, require any answer, at least not till after the death of Sir Timothy Shelley, when perhaps this explanation would have come with better grace; but I trust to your kindness to put my writing now to a good motive. I am, my dear Hunt, yours affectionately and obliged,

MARY WOLLSTONECRAFT SHELLEY

Brighton, 12 August, 1826

My dearest Hunt —

I write to you from an hill almost as high as Albano — but oh how different! Figure to yourself the edge of a naked promontory, composed of a chalk soil without a tree or shrub — but before I describe further, I pause — supposing that you may have visited this bald and glaring spot — or if not, I am, if my very obtuse muse will permit me — about to write an article on my experiences here — which had I the graceful art *some* have of tricking out the same, would be amusing. It will comprise an account of an excursion we have made to Castle Goring — thro' a truly English country. I mean in the best sense of the word — shady lanes, flowery hedges, wooded uplands, rich farms, and rose-bedecked cottages. One village in particular so took our fancy that we mean at the expiration of another week to leave the barrenness and expense of Brighton and to immure ourselves in a pretty little rural lodging in that same place. I will, if you see no objection, send my article to you, and you will contrive to get it inserted for me; in fact my scant purse makes me seriously intend to indite an article or two, if I can be sure that they will be inserted; but it is dispiriting and annoying to write on purpose not to be printed, as our *friend* H. says. I have an idea of another article. I have been reading a book, "The English in Italy" (pray tell me, if you can, who it is by) — very clever, amusing and true. Lady Charlotte Bury has also written one on the same topic, and Lady Oxford too. I think of writing a criticism on these with a few anecdotes of my own as *sauce piquante*. Do you think it will do for the N.M.?

I have seen no one here, for I have not yet called on the Smiths. I shall, however, before we retreat to Swinton. Mrs. Cleveland (Jane's mother) leaves us tomorrow and we expect to be very tranquil. A little amusement to our task would be very acceptable, but since we cannot get that we forge merriment out of dulness itself. You know my Janey's cheerful, gay and contented temper — I cannot be sorrowful while with her — and though with many thoughts to annoy me, I lose, while with her, the dear melancholy that for months has devoured me, and am as gay as herself. I cannot express to you the extreme gratitude I feel towards this darling girl,[1] for the power she has over me of influencing me to happiness. Often when I have spent solitary hours in fruitless and unwise tears, one glance at her dear brow and glad smile has dismissed the

[1] It appears that this "darling girl" proved false. In a journal entry of July 13, 1827, Mrs. Shelley writes — "My friend has proved false and treacherous! Miserable discovery! For four years I was devoted to her, and earned only ingratitude. Not for worlds would I attempt to transfer the deathly blackness of my meditations to these pages. Let no trace remain, save the deep, bleeding, hidden wound of my lost heart, of such a tale of horror and despair." Sometime prior to this, Jane Williams had married T. Jefferson Hogg. Of what her chief treachery consisted we are not told, but it is known that among other things she prated of her great power over Shelley, of his devotion to her, and of Mary's consequent jealousy, all of which claims were unquestionably false. Her husband and Shelley had been bosom friends, and were drowned together.

devils and restored me to pleasurable feeling. She *is* in truth my all, my sole delight — the dear azure sky from which I — a sea of bitterness beneath — catch alien hues and shine reflecting her loveliness. This excessive feeling towards her has grown slowly, but is now a part of myself, and I live to all good and pleasure only thro' her.

How is Marianne? I fear that all has not gone as well with her as it ought. I am anxious to hear the result of her indisposition. How are the Gliddons? — dear and good creatures — how very hard that they who knew so well how to appreciate their happiness and to turn good fortune to good account should be snatched from some of their chief pleasures! Yet while they still enjoy that best gift of heaven — the true *Gliddonic* cheerfulness and good humour, they cannot be so much to be pitied as many better visited by fate. Nor in considering this peculiar and family *attribute* — a special gift of the deity — would I detract from the merit of each and all of them in cultivating this donation. It is so easy to repine, so easy to accuse heaven, earth and the laws of nature; so easy to waste in endless tears and dark grief; but to smile at ill-luck and bear with unaltered brow hateful employments and care for tomorrow — *hic labor hoc opus est* (there is a piece of blueism for you — *true blue* with a false concord, I fear, for I cannot remember the gender of *labor*). God bless them all and help their undertakings. I trust Anne will already have met with an artist who will appreciate her talent and put her in the right way. I am sure that she will succeed in that best and most amiable of all the arts.

I do not think that we shall exceed our time here. I trust that we shall find you on our next walk up the Hill as well as England has made you ever since your return — looking how unlike West's Florentine picture, how unlike when I first saw you in the Vale of Health — better and younger than either. I scratch out because Marianne will laugh and you will think that I am flattering you, which *she* will not. I cannot pretend to say what were the looks of the black muzzled personage, who first cried havoc and let slip the darts of little *Cupid*, but certainly he is ten years younger than he was ten years ago; ten —

no, nine, is it not? — when first, having imaged a kind of fair ruddy light haired radical, I saw in the bust-and-flower-adorned parlour those dark deep eyes looking from under those wise brows — Basta poi — What more? Adieu — the last word of all — Addio — and then a rivederti — dear Italian — how I delight in your . . . . . . — Carissimo Amico — Addio — penii labotta . . . . con tutta quella bontà jolita tua — e l'affezzione dorenta à una che ti amor pur sempre.

God bless you. Embrace your children for me and give an especial kiss to Mary's pretty eyelids, and the smiling mouth of *my* Vincenzo. Occhi Turchini Marianne — is more mine than yours — by *your own confession*. Do you understand Marianne? — God bless you too, dear girl.

Yours affectionately, my kind friends.

MARY SHELLEY

There are in James Street here two neighbouring butchers — one is called Venus and the other Myrtle. This is as bad as the consecration of the Jasmine.

I beg your pardon — I meant to have taken special care in writing to you that

175

my y's were not g's, but I write in haste and console myself with knowing that the worst will be a little laughing and quizzing, which I do not dislike from friends and take no credit for my indifference. It may proceed from vanity — partly it proceeds from satisfaction that while you laugh, nothing very bad is behind in the way of reprehension.

Harrow,[1] 3 February, 1835
My dear Hunt —

Thank you for your kind letter. I hope things are going on as prosperously as you expected. I am glad to hear of dear Henry's destination; he was a very fine boy when I saw him last — and no doubt still *tops* Percy, though for size *round*, I am afraid he must yield.

Believe me, I did not think of currying your public influence for my book when I wrote, for valuable as that is, it did not enter my head. Where the book is, I cannot even imagine; it has been printed these ten months, but I hear nothing of it and can extract no information from

[1] Mary's son Percy was attending Harrow School and she was living there to be near him.

Burlington Street, which I strongly suspect has become a Ward of St. Luke's. A volume of the *Lives* is coming out directly. Is out, that is, on the 1st. Unfortunately, before I was applied to, some of the *best lives* were in other hands. The omnipresent Mr. Montgomery wrote Dante and Ariosto in the present volume; the rest are mine.

I wish I could look with the indulgence you do on Shelley's relations. Sir Tim, indeed, were he alone, I could manage — did I see him — violent as he is, he has a heart and I am sure I could have made a friend of him. It is Lady S[helley] who is my bitter enemy; and her motive is the base one of securing more money for herself, and her terror was great lest I should see Sir Tim at one time. Now there is no fear since the old gentleman never comes to town. Besides the sacra auri fames (is that the right syntax? I wager not) her conduct having been very open to censure, she naturally attacks me, because those kind of women love detraction.

Janey paid me a visit yesterday. She is looking very well; we talked about you — you know how great a favourite you are with her. I had already got the books you mentioned. However defective these lines are (and I am far from satisfied) I spared no pains to get information and to do my best.

I have not been to town for months. I have no idea when I shall visit it again. I am quite a prisoner. I can't tell you how civil and kind the Conservatives have shown themselves about papa's place, which was in jeopardy. The D[uke] of W[ellington] and Sir Robert Peel both have shown the greatest consideration, besides the *real good* of continuing him in it. They have not the *Morgue* of our Whigs. Do write and let me know how you all are. It is too late in the day to congratulate Thornton, but I *do* wish him and Kate all happiness with all my heart. They are both deserving. With love to Marianne and best wishes, I am, dear Hunt,

Sincerely Yours ever,

M. W. SHELLEY

I have mislaid your letter and forget the address. I fear *Chelsea* would not be enough, so send the letter to Mr. Hunter's.

Dear Hunt —

I send you the rest of the Devil that you may judge better. You see I have scratched out a few lines which might be *too shocking;* and yet I hate to *mutilate.* Consider the fate of the book only — if this Essay is to preclude a number of readers who else would snatch at it — for so many of the religious particularly like Shelley — had I better defer the publication till all he has left is published? Let me hear what you think as soon as you can.

Remember Wednesday.

Yours,

M. S.

Putney, Sunday.

Remember *I* do not enter into the question at all. It is *my* duty to publish every thing of Shelley; but I want these two volumes to be popular, and would it be as well to *defer* this Essay?

Send back the slips.

Dear Hunt —

I have desired to fix a day when you will meet Clare, but have not yet been able. I hope I shall soon. Meanwhile I

179

wish much to hear of your Play, and when it will appear.

Percy is very anxious to learn.

I see a few asterisks and omissions in the letters of Shelley you published. Were these wholly private and indifferent, or did some temporary or modest personal reason cause them?

If the latter, pray let me replace them; let me have the originals for a few days — but then it must be *directly*, as they are printing fast off. Tomorrow, it ought to be.

I hope you have been quite well all this time.

Yours truly,

M. W. SHELLEY

Putney, 14th Nov.

Dear Hunt —

Many thanks for your kind note — I have not yet made up my mind. Except that I do not like the idea of a mutilated edition, I have no scruple of conscience in leaving out the expressions which Shelley would never have printed in after life. *I* have a great love for *Queen Mab*. He was proud of it when I first knew him, and it is associated with the bright young days of both of us.

Thanks for your very kind offer of assisting me in my note. But it must rest on myself alone. The edition will be mine; and though I feel my incompetency, yet trying to make it as good as I can, I must hope the best. In a future edition if you will add any of your own peculiarly delightful notes it will make the book more valuable to every reader; but our notes must be independent of each other, for as no two minds exactly agree, so (though in works of imagination two minds may add zest and vivacity) in matters of opinion we should perhaps only spoil both.

Will you look in on me on Tuesday? With love to Marianne,

Ever yours,
M. W. SHELLEY

August 17, '39

Dear Hunt —

I am about to publish a volume of Prose of Shelley's. This will please you, I am sure, and it will not be painful to me, as the other was. But I want your advice on several portions of it, especially with regard to the translation of the Symposium. I want also to know whether you would assent to the letters you published in your Recollections being joined to such as I shall publish.

I expect you on Wednesday and will dine at five; but if you could [come] a little earlier to discuss these things I shall be glad. Do not disappoint me on Wednesday, or you will disappoint Mr. Robinson who *almost* worships you — besides two pretty daughters who have inherited his feeling. You need not be at the trouble of answering this letter. I only write that you may come, if you can, a little earlier, for the reason I have mentioned.

I have read your play — it is admirably written. It is full of beautiful and elevated and true morality clothed in poetry. Yet I can understand Macready's not liking to identify himself with Agolanti; his conduct, true to nature and common, being redeemed by no high self-forgetting passion, would not I think interest in representation as much as in reading. I long to hear of your new play.

Ever truly yours,

M. W. SHELLEY

Putney, Friday.

Putney, 20th April, 1844

My dear Hunt —

The tidings from Field Place seem to say that ere long there will be a change; if nothing untoward happens to us till then, it will be for the better. Twenty years ago, in memory of what Shelley's intentions were, I said that you should be considered one of the legatees to the amount of two thousand pounds. I need scarcely mention that when Shelley talked of leaving you this sum he contemplated reducing other legacies, and that one among them is (by a mistake of the solicitor) just double what he intended it to be.

Twenty years have, of course, much changed my position. Twenty years ago it was supposed that Sir Timothy would not live five years. Meanwhile a large debt has accumulated, for I must pay back all on which Percy and I have subsisted, as well as what I borrowed for Percy's going to college. In fact, I scarcely know how our affairs will be. Moreover, Percy shares now my right; that promise was made without his concurrence, and he must concur to render it of avail. Nor do I like to ask him to do so till our affairs are

183

so settled that we know what we shall have — whether Shelley's uncle may not go to law; in short, till we see our way before us.

It is both my and Percy's great wish to feel that you are no longer so burdened by care and necessity; in that he is as desirous as I can be; but the form and the degree in which we can do this must at first be uncertain. From the time of Sir Timothy's death [1] I shall give directions to my banker to honour your quarterly cheques for thirty pounds a quarter; and I shall take steps to secure this to you, and to Marianne if she should survive you.

Percy has read this letter, and approves. I know your *real* delicacy about money matters, and that you will at once be ready to enter into my views; and feel assured that if any present debt should press, if we have any command of money, we will take care to free you from it.

With love to Marianne, affectionately yours,

MARY SHELLEY

[1] Sir Timothy died in the same month this letter was written, and Leigh Hunt received thereafter one hundred and twenty pounds a year as long as he lived.

41d Park St., Friday

I will give your message to Jane,[1] but to poor pedestrian ladies, Chelsea is *very* far — especially in winter, or we should have called before.

The following summary is taken from Mary Shelley's journal, October 21, 1838: —

"I have been so often abused by pretended friends for my lukewarmness in 'the good cause,' that I disdain to answer them. I shall put down here a few thoughts on this subject. I am much of a self-examiner. Vanity is not my fault, I think; if it is, it is uncomfortable vanity, for I have none that teaches me to be satisfied with myself; far otherwise — and, if I use the word disdain, it is that I think my qualities (such as they are) not appreciated from unworthy causes. In the first place, with regard to 'the good cause' — the cause of advancement of freedom and knowledge, of the rights of women, etc. — I am not a person of opinions. I have said elsewhere that human beings differ

---

[1] Whether or not this is Jane Williams it does not appear. Possibly they may have made up their differences. In 1835 she wrote Hunt that "Janey" had paid her a visit.

greatly in this. Some have a passion for reforming the world, others do not cling to particular opinions. That my parents and Shelley were of the former class makes me respect it. I respect such when joined to real disinterestedness, toleration, and a clear understanding. My accusers, after such as these, appear to me mere drivellers. For myself, I earnestly desire the good and enlightenment of my fellow-creatures, and see all, in the present course, tending to the same, and rejoice; but I am not for violent extremes, which only bring on an injurious reaction. I have never written a word in disfavour of liberalism; that I have not supported it openly in writing arises from the following causes, as far as I know —

That I have not argumentative powers: I see things pretty clearly, but cannot demonstrate them. Besides, I feel the counter-arguments too strongly. I do not feel that I could say aught to support the cause efficiently; besides that, on some topics (especially with regard to my own sex) I am far from making up my mind. I believe we are sent here to educate ourselves, and that self-denial, and disappointment, and self-control are a part of our education; that it is not by taking away all restraining law that our improvement is to be achieved; and, though many things need great amendment, I can by no means go so far as my friends would have me. When I feel that I can say what will benefit my fellow-creatures, I will speak; not before. Then, I recoil from the vulgar abuse of the inimical press. I do more than recoil: proud and sensitive, I act on the defensive — an inglorious position. To hang back, as I do, brings a penalty. I was nursed and fed with a love of glory. To be something great and good was the precept given me by my father; Shelley reiterated it. Alone and poor, I could only be something by joining a party; and there was much in me — the woman's love of looking up, and being guided, and being willing to do anything if any one supported and brought me forward — which would have made me a good partisan. But Shelley died and I was alone. My father, from age and domestic circumstances, could not *me faire valoir*. My total friendlessness, my horror of pushing, and inability to put myself forward unless led, cherished and supported — all this has sunk me in a state of loneliness no other human being ever before, I believe, endured — except Robinson Crusoe. How many tears and spasms of anguish this solitude has cost me, lies buried in my memory.

If I had raved and ranted about what I did not understand, had I adopted a set of opinions, and propagated them with enthusiasm; had I been careless of attack, and eager for notoriety; then the party to which I belonged had gathered round me, and I had not been alone.

It has been the fashion with these same friends to accuse me of worldliness. There, indeed, in my own heart and conscience, I take a high ground. I may distrust my own judgment too much — be too indolent and too timid; but in conduct I am above merited blame.

I like society; I believe all persons who have any talent (who are in good health) do. The soil that gives forth nothing may lie ever fallow; but that which produces — however humble its product — needs cultivation, change of harvest, refreshing dews, and ripening sun. Books do much; but the living intercourse is the vital heat. Debarred from that, how have I pined and died!

My early friends chose the position of enemies. When I first discovered that a trusted friend had acted falsely by me, I was nearly destroyed. My health was shaken. I remember thinking, with a burst of agonising tears, that I should prefer a bed of torture to the unutterable anguish a friend's falsehood engendered. There is no resentment; but the world can never be to me what it was before. Trust and confidence, and the heart's sincere devotion are gone.

I sought at that time to make acquaintances — to divert my mind from this anguish. I got entangled in various ways through my ready sympathy and too eager heart; but I never crouched to society — never sought it unworthily. If I have never written to vindicate the rights of women, I have ever befriended women when oppressed. At every risk I have befriended and supported victims to the social system; but I make no boast, for in truth it is simple justice I perform; and so I am still reviled for being worldly.

God grant a happier and a better day is near! Percy — my all-in-all — will, I trust, by his excellent understanding, his clear, bright, sincere spirit and affectionate heart, repay me for sad long years of desolation. His career may lead me into the thick of life or only gild a quiet home. I am content with either, and, as I grow older, I grow more fearless for myself — I become firmer in my opinions. The experienced, the suffering, the thoughtful, may at last speak unrebuked. If it be the will of God that I live, I may ally my name yet to "the Good Cause," though I do not expect to please my accusers.

Thus have I put down my thoughts. I may have deceived myself; I may be in the wrong; I try to examine myself; and such as I have written appears to me the exact truth.

Enough of this! The great work of life goes on. Death draws near. To be better after death than in life is one's hope and endeavour — to be so through self-schooling. If I write the above, it is that those who love me may hereafter know that I am not all to blame, nor merit the heavy accusations cast on me for not

putting myself forward. I cannot do that;
it is against my nature. As well cast me
from a precipice and rail at me for not
flying."

The remainder of Mary Shelley's life
was passed quietly; it was devoted to the
education of her son and to the memory
of her husband, who she insisted was not
dead, but was only waiting for her to join
him in another sphere. She wrote —

My trembling hand shall never write thee — dead —
Thou liv'st in Nature, Love, My Memory,
With deathless faith for aye adoring thee,
The wife of Time no more, I wed Eternity.

On February 21, 1851, her soul took
flight to join him in another sphere.

Printed in the United States
129329LV00003B/106/A